DEAN W. COLVARD
Quiet Leader

MARION A. ELLIS

DEAN W.

COLVARD
Quiet Leader

University of North Carolina at Charlotte
Charlotte, North Carolina

Design and production by BW&A Books, Inc.,
Durham, North Carolina
Typeset in Cycles and Bell
Printed in the United States of America
by Edwards Brothers, Inc., Lillington, North Carolina

The paper in this book meets the guidelines for permanence
and durability of the Committee on Production Guidelines
for Book Longevity of the Council on Library Resources.

Library of Congress Cataloging-in-Publication Data
Ellis, Marion A.
Dean W. Colvard : quiet leader / Marion A. Ellis.
  p. cm.
Includes index.
ISBN: 0-945344-05-8 (cloth : alk. paper)
1. Colvard, Dean W., 1913– 2. Mississippi State
University—Presidents—Biography. 3. University
of North Carolina at Charlotte—Biography.
4. College administrators—North Carolina—
Charlotte—Biography. I. Title.
LD3381.M617C654 2004
378.1'11'092—dc22
[B]   2004044075

5   4   3   2   1

CONTENTS

FOREWORD

Higher education is one of America's most celebrated success stories. The United States is currently the richest, most envied nation in the world, largely because over the past three centuries it has invested heavily in the education of great masses of its people. In doing so, it also has made higher education one of America's greatest exports. The story of American higher education's rise to international prominence can be told in the ever-increasing commitment of churches, states, and local and federal governments to extending educational opportunity to an expanding proportion of the American people. It also is the story of the visionary men and women who harnessed those church and government programs and used them to advantage in developing great colleges and universities.

This book is the story of one of those visionary men and women. Dean Wallace Colvard began life in the remote mountains of North Carolina. He saw education as his personal path for escaping the cruel confines of rural poverty. In becoming a teacher, researcher, administrator, and university executive, he devoted a lifetime to making similar educational opportunities available to thousands of others. His personal rise to prominence at Berea College, at Brevard Junior College, at the University of Missouri, at a test farm at Swannanoa in North Carolina, then at Purdue University, NC State, Mississippi State, and finally at UNC Charlotte, closely parallels the rise of American higher education in the twentieth century.

We at UNC Charlotte are grateful to all of those people and institutions that have contributed to the compiling and publishing of this biography. We especially thank the leaders of Mississippi State University for their cooperation and encouragement. We are grateful to our many friends at NC State, who share our admiration for Dean Colvard. We are grateful to the many people at UNC Charlotte who told of their involvement with Dean Colvard and his family. And we thank the many contributors to the UNC Charlotte Foundation, under whose auspices the publication of this book was financed.

We are especially grateful to Dean and Martha Colvard for their willingness to open their lives, to reveal their personal records, and to disclose some of their most intimate family moments in order to bring this book into being.

The biography is intended to be an inspiration to other men and women who, facing limitations in life, might find joy and encouragement in the story of this exemplary man.

James H. Woodward
Chancellor, University of North Carolina at Charlotte

FOREWORD

Mississippi State University has been led by seventeen presidents during its 125 years, but none served at a more critical moment in the history of the institution or left a more lasting imprint than Dean Wallace Colvard. Although he headed MSU for only six years before leaving Mississippi nearly four decades ago, he is widely remembered as the individual who, perhaps more than any other, began the transition that led to a modern, comprehensive university.

Marion Ellis has succinctly captured Dr. Colvard's genius for low-key but effective leadership, his knack for identifying talent, and his ability to elicit the best from those around him. Nowhere in a long and productive career were these traits more evident or put to better use than during Dr. Colvard's six years in Mississippi.

Taking office only two years after Mississippi State College became Mississippi State University, he presided over a period of growth and change perhaps unequaled before or since in the life of the institution. Dr. Colvard began by reshaping the administration, and the outlines of the structure he created remain visible today. He gave prominence and importance to research and graduate education, strengthened the credentials of the faculty, and initiated an extensive building program. He was the catalyst for the university's entry into the realm of private fund-raising, which has since become vital to public institutions. He helped articulate the university's critical role in the economic development of the state.

Famously, he shepherded Mississippi State through some of the most tense moments of the struggle for civil rights, ensuring that the 1965 integration of the university was remarkably uneventful, allowing the institution more fully to embrace its traditional mission as "the People's University," and helping Mississippi to move toward overcoming its history of racial turmoil.

Less tangibly, but no less importantly for that, Dr. Colvard helped Mississippi State, its faculty, its students, its alumni, and its constituents throughout the state to raise their expectations of their university and of themselves. He saw Mississippi State for what it could become as much as for what it was, and he enabled others to share his vision.

The man, the place, and the time were ideally matched when Dr. Colvard came to Mississippi State in 1960, and the resulting chemistry continues to yield benefits for all of the citizens of this state. Perhaps no university in the country is as important to the future of its state as Mississippi State is to Mississippi, and perhaps no individual has done more than Dean Wallace Colvard to help the university find its direction and fulfill its purpose.

J. Charles Lee
President, Mississippi State University

ACKNOWLEDGMENTS

During the three years I spent writing this book, I came to know why his friends and coworkers called Dean Colvard the quiet leader. It was because of his calm, deliberative way of inspiring others to excel, but not only for that. He never tried to grab the spotlight. He was a man who lived by the credo: "It is amazing how much can be done if you do not mind who gets the credit." He trained three generations of leaders in higher education not only to lead, but to lead boldly, to know that success sometimes meant taking risks. He was a man who respected and revered the past but never let it dictate his future.

When I began this project in March 2000, I truly had no idea how brilliant and creative a leader Dr. Colvard had been during his time in higher education. All I knew was that he had been the first chancellor of the new University of North Carolina at Charlotte in 1966, but I mistakenly had assumed that his role there was as a perfunctory bureaucrat, simply following orders from headquarters. It was not until I had completed much research that I began to get the full and true picture of his imaginative and courageous leadership in building the state's fourth public university campus and in many other endeavors for the public good.

During the course of this research, which involved interviews with dozens of leaders in higher education, business, and politics in North Carolina, Mississippi, Missouri, and Kentucky, I began to take on a new appreciation of Dr. Colvard's abilities. I learned that he had to overcome many obstacles in his long career at NC State, Mississippi State, and UNCC, but I never heard one hint of regret, not one tinge of bitterness, not one shadow of a doubt from his lips in hundreds of hours I spent with him.

He truly was a man of drive and determination, but one who let his actions speak for themselves, perhaps sometimes to his own detriment. He often let others take center stage when he could rightfully have claimed that spotlight for himself.

His true friends and followers, the legions of loyal workers he left behind, know the truth, and now so do I.

I am grateful to many for their cooperation in being able to complete this biography of Dr. Dean Wallace Colvard. They are far too numerous to list here, but I must mention a few: Martha Colvard, who became Mrs. Dean W. Colvard in 1939; Ben Romine of Tryon, North Carolina; Jack Claiborne of Charlotte; Elaine Deese of UNCC; Chester McKee of Starkville, Mississippi; George Rent of Mississippi State University; and finally Ken Sanford, whose *Charlotte and UNC Charlotte: Growing Up Together* (1996) has been an invaluable resource in the writing of this book.

DEAN W. COLVARD

Quiet Leader

INTRODUCTION

Coming out of the mountains of North Carolina in the early twentieth century when times were hard and the future looked bleak, Dean W. Colvard overcame many obstacles to emerge as a national leader in higher education.

Rarely does a person get a chance to help shape one great public university, but Colvard helped build three—North Carolina State University, Mississippi State University, and finally the University of North Carolina at Charlotte.

After serving as dean of agriculture at North Carolina State, Colvard moved on in 1960 to become president of Mississippi State University. In that post, he led the way in March 1963 in overturning Mississippi's "unwritten law" against having athletic teams play against integrated teams, and in 1965 he was at the helm when Mississippi State admitted its first African American student, without a hint of the type of trouble that had erupted three years earlier at the University of Mississippi.

Writer Alexander Wolff recounted the 1963 triumph in a major article in the March 10, 2003, issue of *Sports Illustrated,* saying that "Colvard, a political and temperamental moderate from North Carolina," was alone responsible for "the decision to defy the extreme segregationists."

The magazine devoted ten pages to the event, with the headline "Ghosts of Mississippi." The article began, "Forty years ago a courageous college president defied a court order barring Mississippi State from integrated competition and sent his team to face black players in the NCAA tournament."

Colvard would stay at Mississippi State for six years before moving back to his native North Carolina to become the first chancellor of the new University of North Carolina at Charlotte.

When Colvard went to Mississippi State, Mississippi was still far behind other southern states in race relations. Despite the 1954 U.S. Supreme Court order to integrate the nation's public schools, the ruling had had little effect six years later in Mississippi or in its colleges

1

and universities. Conversely the ruling had caused the creation of private white-only academies, emboldened by a new constitutional amendment authorizing the closing of all public schools rather than having them integrated. Public schools remained separated by race as they always had, despite a number of challenges, most still winding their way through the courts.

The legislature repealed the state law requiring public school attendance, voted that it did not have to obey federal laws, and created the State Sovereignty Commission to be a watchdog against all attempts at integration.

From his professorial appearance, Colvard looked nothing like the type of person who would confront the governor, much less put his job on the line over a principle involving race relations. Colvard looked as if he might be an accountant, not a social firebrand. His horn-rimmed eyeglasses and square jaw made him appear attentive and contemplative, not action oriented, more of an Eisenhower or Truman than a Kennedy. He exuded a quiet confidence. But throughout his long career Colvard would prove again and again that appearances can be deceiving. Underneath that calm exterior lay the tenacious spirit of a bulldog, the mascot Colvard found at Mississippi State.

Mississippi State needed and wanted Colvard because of his background in agricultural science and academic administration. After years of somnolence and legislative neglect, the college in Starkville had only recently been given university status, and the newly aware legislature had begun to pump substantial amounts of state money into it, recognizing finally that the research and teaching functions of the school could bring great benefits to the state.

Colvard had grown up in the mountains of North Carolina, where there were very few black people and consequently few outward signs of the deep, pervasive prejudice found in most of the South. He had graduated from Berea College in Kentucky and shared that institution's liberal stance on racial relationships. However, Colvard did not consider himself what some called an integrationist. His attitude could have been categorized as moderate, leaning toward following the federal law and treating everyone, including African Americans, with fairness, not harshness.

But he knew he was coming into his new job at Mississippi State as an outsider, and he was determined to make no major controversial moves until he had built a solid following among not only the university types, but also the business and agricultural leadership and the community in general.

Little did Colvard know that his academic accomplishments at MSU, as great as they would become, would pale in the light of his accomplishments in the field of race relations and human relations. By the time he left to become the first chancellor of Charlotte's new university, he would have shown Mississippians the way to change the state's image and establish MSU as one of the outstanding research centers in the South.

When Colvard returned to North Carolina, tiny Charlotte College, which had been formed in downtown Charlotte from an old high school to serve returning World War II veterans, existed no more. Instead the North Carolina legislature had created the fourth branch of the University of North Carolina, locating it in a few nondescript buildings in a cow pasture nine miles northeast of the center city. His appointment as chancellor at the fourth branch of the University of North Carolina was not popular with many in Charlotte who felt that the post should have gone to a woman named Bonnie Cone, a tireless promoter of Charlotte College since its beginning. But Cone had no earned doctorate and had never led a major university; Colvard had both, two key ingredients needed to build a new institution. Despite the controversy, Colvard used his management and administrative abilities to win over Cone and allow her to use her experience and expertise to help the new university become a major force in higher education in the state.

By the time he retired in 1978, Colvard could report that enrollment had grown from 1,715 students to 8,504 and faculty from 99 to 378, with 85 percent holding doctoral degrees. Colvard directed an annual budget that had grown to $18.6 million, and he could point with pride to other accomplishments as well. The UNCC Foundation's assets had grown to $2,517,116. Endowments held directly by the university totaled $677,460, and trusts that would accrue to it were more than $850,000.

Undergraduate degree programs had gone from eighteen to thirty-four and graduate programs from zero to ten. The number of volumes in the library had soared from 60,000 to 275,000. The value of the physical plant had gone from $8.1 million to more than $54 million and the square footage in use or under construction from 355,633 to 1,557,313, with another seven buildings with 211,995 square feet authorized.

In 1976, two years before Colvard retired, the newly elected governor of North Carolina, James B. Hunt, asked him to join him as his chief of staff, but Colvard graciously declined because he could not leave his job at UNCC unfinished.

After his retirement from UNCC, Colvard took on a number of important, substantial assignments, including supervision of the beginning of North Carolina's outstanding School of Science and Mathematics at Durham. He also continued to serve in various capacities at each of the great universities, whenever called upon to do so.

What were some of the influences on this man who came from modest circumstances to become one of the South's outstanding academic leaders?

First of all, those modest circumstances taught him the value of honest, hard work. Growing up during the Great Depression taught him how to preserve scarce resources and how to be resourceful with whatever assets you may possess.

Colvard was a perfect product of the age of boundless optimism during the 1920s, followed by the age of hard knocks during the 1930s, shaped by the effects of two World Wars and their subsequent boom times. But he learned to emulate his heroes: his father; the president of Berea College; North Carolina Governor W. Kerr Scott; and the academic giant of the times, Frank Porter Graham, who took over as president of the University of North Carolina in 1931, in the heart of the Depression.

Colvard personified the North Carolina motto *esse quam videri,* "to be rather than to seem."

This book is but a brief summation of Dean W. Colvard's long career in higher education and public service.

UNC Charlotte and UNCC are used interchangeably throughout the book.

PART 1

1 "MOUNTAIN BOYS DON'T MIND A LITTLE SCRAP"

Sixteen-year-old Dean Colvard had a dilemma in the spring of 1930. He wanted a class ring to mark his high school graduation, but there was no way his family could afford the $12.50 price tag.

In the hardscrabble life of the Blue Ridge Mountains in the Great Depression, it had been no small feat for Colvard to take care of all his chores on the family farm, walk two and a half miles each way to and from school, and do his homework by the light of a kerosene lamp. Colvard had scrimped and saved. He had taken every odd job he could find, which was not many since there was little spare money to pay him. He had trapped rabbits and sold them. He had collected mountain herbs of galax and murdock and sold them at the country store. But still there was not enough cash in his pocket.

Finally, he concluded that he would have to sell his favored black-and-tan hunting hound to get enough money to buy the ring. He hated to part with the eight-month-old dog because he was one of the best trackers of wild game in the Grassy Creek community. "I loved that little dog," Colvard could still recall many years later. "If I had not been planning on getting away from home after graduation, I would not have sold him." The price—$12.50.

The story is an excellent illustration of the measure of the man—determined to succeed and resourceful enough to find a way to do it.

Dean Colvard came to know the real value of a dollar earned through hard work. He learned that neighbors helped each other—at harvest-time, barn buildings, and in times of crisis. He was taught to make the best of what nature provided—both wild and homegrown meat and poultry, vegetables, and fruit to eat, wood to burn, animal skins and wild herbs to sell.

Chopping firewood for the cold winter and other chores taught him to be prepared, to take the initiative rather than wait for events to overwhelm him. All these were valuable lessons that Colvard passed along to coworkers during his long and varied career as an educator and top administrator.

Dean Colvard had good role models in his mother and father. Mary Elizabeth Shepherd was seventeen years old when, on March 30, 1910, she married twenty-eight-year-old Wiley Pinkney Colvard, whose forebears had lived in the Wilkes County area since the 1770s. The ceremony took place before her parents in the living room of the bride's home on a farm near Crumpler in Ashe County, North Carolina, about three miles from the Colvard farm. Colvard had four Wilkes County friends as his witnesses. There was no honeymoon, and the groom went to work the next day preparing the soil for a corn crop on his parents' home place. A year later, the young couple moved into a log house on seventy acres in nearby Ashe County, and this was where their first child, Ruby Hazeline, was born on May 4, 1911. The new place was in a beautiful and peaceful area known as the Grassy Creek community. You will not find it on most maps of North Carolina. It is just a tiny community nestled in the Blue Ridge Mountains straddling the North Carolina–Virginia line about twelve miles north of Jefferson, North Carolina. Grassy Creek winds its way through the rolling hills for about four miles before it flows into the north fork of the New River.

With the help of local carpenters and laborers, Wiley had logs sawed into planks at a sawmill and built a two-story, six-room house. And that was where Dean Wallace Colvard was born on July 10, 1913, the second child and first son. There was no significance to his name Dean; his mother just liked the sound of it. He was followed by another boy, Charles Deward, and four girls, Mary Arleine, Mabel Virginia, Audrey Leah, and Carol Wade.

"It was not an easy life, but fortunately I was taught to make the best of what I had, and I never felt mistreated or permanently repressed by the hardships," Colvard wrote in his unpublished autobiography, *Education Was My Ticket*. He and his brother took turns every morning, even on those cold winter ones, starting the fires in the downstairs fireplace and wood-burning cook stove. "On a typical day we got out of bed in an unheated room at about five in the morning, went down-stairs barefooted, and got the fires going," Colvard wrote. "Afterwards we dressed, lit a lantern and checked our traps to see if we had caught any rabbits, opossums or other game. On our return to the barn, we helped our father feed the cattle and horses and milk the cows." Dean and his brother also gathered chestnuts when they could to sell at a local grocery, but they had to get out to the fields very early or the wild turkeys would beat them to the nuts. "I never figured out how a turkey could eat a chestnut," Colvard recalled years later.

When he was six years old, Dean had been sent on the two-and-a-half mile ride to school on a horse behind his sister Ruby. The wood-frame school building housed all eleven grades and straddled the North Carolina–Virginia line. The government of Virginia supported the lower grades, and North Carolina was responsible for the upper, called Virginia-Carolina High School. The boys played baseball in a field where the pitcher hurled from the mound in Virginia and the catcher was in North Carolina. Dean played center field because he could throw out runners at home plate. He and the other boys didn't have uniforms. They just wore their regular bib overalls and flannel shirts. On their feet were the standard brown leather high-top brogans that all farm boys wore. The lack of athletic shoes kept action at a minimum on the out-door basketball court, and football was not played at all.

Dean was a quiet, studious, hardworking boy who loved to play checkers and read books like Zane Grey westerns. On his birthday, his mother would make his favorite dessert, chocolate cream pie. He and his brother loved to go fishing with their dad when they could. The Colvard boys helped their father eke out a living by selling a few calves, poultry, eggs, and milk and raising corn and other crops. But their father also took on other jobs to make ends meet. Although he had little education, he was very good with figures, so he was often called on to help area merchants take inventory, and he did some land surveying since he had somehow accumulated the equipment and know-how. He also wrangled an appointment as a local magistrate, which meant he could write deeds and handle other minor legal matters. Because of this honor, the local residents called him "Squire."

Since ministers were scarce in Grassy Creek, Squire Colvard was called on occasionally to perform marriages. Dean Colvard remem-bered his father telling him of the time a young couple drove up to the country store in a Model-T Ford looking for the magistrate so they could get married. "They were in a hurry and Dad agreed to marry them," Colvard recalled. "They were sitting in a car. He said, 'How about backing up a little bit into the State of North Carolina?' That was so he could legally marry them."

Wiley Colvard taught his boys how to hunt, fish, and trap small animals and how to use a shotgun and a rifle at an early age. He told his sons that if he ever heard of them shooting into a covey of quail on the ground, their privilege of using guns would be restricted.

Mary Colvard and the girls usually took care of all the household duties, including cooking, canning, and quilting. As a consequence, Dean never learned to cook; once when he was home alone he made a mess when he tried to fry an egg by putting it on top of the stove without using a frying pan. His mother also kept a large vegetable garden, grew flowers, including a Christmas cactus, and proved to be a crack shot with a rifle, shooting weasels trying to make off with some of the family's chickens or turkeys. In addition to corn and other crops, the Colvard farm provided apples, plums, cherries, peaches, raspberries, and strawberries.

The family attended the New River Baptist Church, but Dean was the only one who never became a member. "I was not against the church, but I was not readily absorbed by the emotional kind of religious activities that occurred there—shouting and immersion in the river and that sort of thing, although I went to Sunday School regularly," he said years later. "I don't really know why I didn't join that church. I did like to go to the black church sometimes because I liked the singing."

Only a few black people, most direct descendants of slaves, lived in the Grassy Creek area, so Dean grew up thinking they were just plain folks who happened to be of a different color. Although they were poor, so was everybody else. "The black men had grubbed stumps side by side with me when I was large enough to help," Colvard recalled. "The women were good friends and always displayed maternalistic concern for me. It was true that they did not sit beside us at our dinner table, but they shared the same food, frequently in the same room."

Wiley Colvard told Dean he wanted him to be an engineer and since he loved bluegrass music he hoped that Dean would learn to play the fiddle. Neither ambition was fulfilled because Dean eventually displayed no musical talent. Instead, Dean became interested in vocational agriculture, primarily because his high school had an excellent teacher, C. A. Jackson, a North Carolina State College graduate, who took students on trips to judge beef cattle competitions. In Dean's junior year, William C. LaRue became the teacher because the State of Virginia had taken over the program. LaRue was a graduate of Virginia Polytechnic Institute in Blacksburg, and that was where he took his students for agricultural contests. It was on one of these trips that Dean Colvard won first place in beef cattle judging in Virginia, beating out seven hundred other boys and getting his photograph in the local weekly newspapers. Colvard also won a gold medal in oratory and played in a few of the Virginia-Carolina High School's dramas.

As Dean approached graduation, he wanted to go on to college, preferably to VPI or NC State, but there was no money, so he found a job with a construction crew in West Virginia. "I was assigned as water boy to carry pails of water from a spring saturated with sulphur," Colvard recalled. "At first I could hardly bear to smell the water, much less drink it." He lasted only two weeks before going back home, then he was off to Maryland, where a cousin got him a job picking apples and husking corn on a big farm until the end of the harvesting season.

"By this time, I was more than ever convinced that I had to find some way to get more education," he wrote in his autobiography. Back home another cousin, who was a teacher, told him about Berea College in nearby Kentucky, where a student could work his way through. Berea had been founded in 1855 as a religious-based but nondenominational school for low-income students from Appalachia. Students accepted at Berea would pay no tuition, but would have to work at jobs that sustained the college.

He applied and was told he lacked a geometry course, but officials at his old high school arranged for him to take a special course. He took only that course that year. "With my light schedule I did not have to go to school every day and had more time to help on the farm and enjoy more social activities at school," Colvard wrote. By the next fall, he was safely enrolled at Berea with $100 that his father had been able to save for his expenses. "I was scared that I might not be able to measure up but exhilarated with the opportunity to try," Colvard remembered.

In the fall of 1931 the Great Depression was in full force, but Colvard believed he was one of the luckiest men alive. He was in college and had a job working in the Berea College creamery. "On a normal day I went to the creamery at 4:30 or 5:00 in the morning to help receive milk coming in from the area farms," Colvard recalled. "Breakfast was sent from the boarding hall to the creamery so I could receive the milk and eat breakfast before classes began." He had a butter mold made that read: "Made by Dean Colvard, Grassy Creek, NC."

Colvard's hard work soon led him to success at Berea. At the end of his freshman year, he ranked fourth in a class of 292, seventeenth in the entire school, and was awarded a full scholarship for his sophomore year, which meant all expenses of $158.40. If his academic record remained satisfactory, his scholarship was to continue through his junior and senior years. He worked his way up in the creamery, where he washed milk cans for eleven cents an hour. He also took on jobs as a lab assistant in zoology and as a clerk in the college business office. As if that was not enough, he collected cleaning orders from students and received free cleaning in return. He and his roommate, Gilbert Hibbard, became good friends and played handball at night in the gymnasium. Later Dean helped pay the bills at Berea for his brother and three of his sisters.

Colvard was impressed with the dedication of his teachers and the president, William J. Hutchins, who was the father of Robert Hutchins, the president of the University of Chicago. Berea's Hutchins helped Colvard make up his mind about a future career when he asked if he would rather work with people or things, and Colvard answered people. Colvard also was impressed with H. E. Taylor, who had made his fortune on Wall Street and had come to Berea as a "dollar-a-year" business manager. Taylor handed him a dictionary one day and asked him to look up the words impossible and worry. "There was a little rectangular hole where the words were supposed to be," Colvard recalled. "The words 'impossible' and 'worry' were not in his dictionary."

At Berea, Colvard met Martha Lampkin, a pretty biology major from Jefferson City, Missouri, who was a class ahead. They never dated each other, but they were good friends and were frequently together in groups.

Upon graduation in 1935, Colvard applied for research assistantships at several universities, but after receiving no offers, he took a job at Brevard Junior College in the Smoky Mountains of North Carolina as instructor–farm manager and director of student work programs. His salary was $100 per month, plus room and board, plenty for the times.

One week after commencement exercises at Berea, Colvard took a bus to Brevard and reported for work. "I was young, energetic, ambitious and highly motivated to develop a career and prove myself," Colvard recalled. He plunged into the work and within a few months had succeeded. One of his coups came after he wrote a letter to Harvey Firestone, founder of the tire and rubber company in Akron, Ohio, to ask him to donate a set of rubber tires for the college's dilapidated tractor, and Firestone came through. These were the first rubber tires most students and local people had seen on a tractor. He had not really expected his request to succeed. But when Firestone came through the young teacher had learned a lesson—that you never know what you can do until you try.

After two years at Brevard, Colvard heard from a former teacher at Berea that a graduate assistantship was available at the University of Missouri at Columbia. He applied and received the award of $600 per year. At Mizzou, Colvard studied the effect of temperature on the reproductive capability of four different breeds of sheep. Most of his time he spent hunched over a microscope comparing specimens. Meanwhile, he had reconnected with Martha Lampkin, who was working as a medical technologist in Kansas City, Missouri.

Within the year, Colvard had decided he did not want to spend the rest of his life looking through microscopes, so he cut short his idea of going directly for a Ph.D. Instead, he received his master's degree in animal physiology in 1938 and began looking for a job that would give him time to reevaluate the direction of his career.

As luck would have it, he had kept in touch with his old boss, Dr. E. J. Coltrane, the president of Brevard Junior College, whose brother David Coltrane had been named assistant to North Carolina Commissioner of Agriculture W. Kerr Scott. E. J. Coltrane offered him a job to return to Brevard, and Scott offered him one as superintendent of the state's agricultural test farm at Swannanoa, near Asheville. The twenty-six-year-old Colvard opted for the Swannanoa job. He soon found it was a controversial move, since he would be displacing a man who had been superintendent there for twenty-one years.

Colvard wondered if the appointment carried political overtones and informed Scott during an interview that he did not play politics. In his characteristically blunt manner, Scott replied, "Now Colvard, I have always heard that you mountain boys don't mind a little scrap. You do a good job for me and that will be the best politics you can play." Scott, a rough-hewn farmer from Alamance County, North Carolina, had taken his degree at NC State where he excelled in track, YMCA work, and debate. He had succeeded his father as a leader in the state Grange and was elected state agriculture commissioner in 1936.

Colvard was to take his new job on July 1, 1938. In the meantime, he had visited Martha Lampkin in Kansas City both while he was in Missouri and after he had returned to North Carolina. They arranged to meet in Chicago on Thanksgiving 1938 and agreed to be married on July 7, 1939, in the chapel at Berea College.

The Swannanoa experimental station was an adjunct operation of the agriculture school at North Carolina State College in Raleigh. The college was getting special attention because Frank Porter Graham, president of the University of North Carolina since 1930 and a powerful education figure, had decided it should become a national leader in agricultural education and research.

Colvard recalled a vivid memory he had of his first fortunate acquaintance with Graham. In August 1939 he and his bride of less than a year met Graham at the Swannanoa railroad station and drove him in their second-hand Plymouth to Berea College, three hundred miles away. Graham delivered an erudite and lengthy inauguration address to install Dr. Francis Hutchins as the new president of the college. In the two days of the round trip, Colvard and Graham started to build a relationship that lasted for decades. Unknown to Colvard, before the Kentucky trip, Dr. Clarence Poe, editor of the *Progressive Farmer* magazine and a member of Graham's university executive committee, had sent Graham a copy of a letter that Colvard had written bemoaning the fact that no state university in the Southeast offered a Ph.D. in animal sciences. Graham undoubtedly had read the letter and decided to ride with Colvard so they could discuss Colvard's observation.

Graham had called on his considerable powers of persuasion with the legislature to start to build the agricultural education program at NC State, but that was not enough, so he forged a connection with the Rockefeller Foundation's General Education Board, which began to funnel money into NC State as part of an effort to improve agriculture in the South. Graham convinced the organization to use some of that money as salary supplements to attract bright, capable, and well-known Ph.D.s in their fields from leading agricultural universities across the nation to Raleigh to begin to build a national power there. The Rockefeller Foundation agreed to give NC State $50,000 to supplement salaries of faculty members if matching funds could be found. Graham convinced NC State alumnus and tobacco heir Richard J. Reynolds, Jr., in Winston-Salem to provide the matching funds.

Graham was known as a tireless and persuasive president. Born on October 14, 1886, in Fayetteville, North Carolina, Graham came from a family of distinguished educators. A 1909 graduate of UNC, he had attended the university's law school for a year and taught high school for a year. He then resumed his law studies and was admitted to the bar, although he never practiced. He went on to Columbia University, where he received his master's degree in history in 1916. After serving in the Marines in World War I, the ruggedly handsome and personable Graham taught at UNC briefly and then studied at the University of Chicago, the Brookings Institution, and the University of London. He returned to Chapel Hill in 1925 to teach history and in June 1930 was named university president, although he never received a Ph.D. (Later he was addressed as Dr. Frank Porter Graham because of numerous honorary doctorate degrees.) When the three campuses at Raleigh, Chapel Hill, and Greensboro were merged in 1931, Graham was named the leader of the new consolidated university system. A sometimes controversial leader throughout the South in human relations because of his liberal views, considered socialist by some, he was to stay at UNC until 1949 when he was appointed to the U.S. Senate to serve out the term of J. Melville Broughton, who had died in office.

Graham was president during the tough times of the Great Depression when the university's budget was cut to the bone, and during the boom times following World War II when thousands of veterans were returning to college and the demand for expanded facilities of every type was at its peak. Even before the postwar boom, Graham envisioned the university becoming an instrumental force in helping pull North Carolina agriculture out of the mule-and-plow days by using the very latest technology in plant and animal science. Graham's ambition for the university knew no bounds. Although UNC consisted of only three institutions with a combined student body of less than 6,000, Graham predicted in his 1933 annual report that consolidation of the three campuses under one administration eventually "will make possible the development in North Carolina as one of the great intellectual and spiritual centers of the world."

His role in developing NC State into an agricultural academic powerhouse was highlighted in 1940 when the *Progressive Farmer* magazine named him its Man of the Year in North Carolina.

Graham recruited Dr. Robert M. Salter from Ohio State University to become NC State's director of research, but Salter said he would accept the job if he could bring Dr. Leonard D. Baver with him from Ohio State to become head of the agronomy department. An Ohio native, Salter had received his bachelor's degree from Ohio State, his master's from West Virginia University, and his doctorate from the University of Missouri. Baver also hailed from Ohio and had received his bachelor's and master's from Ohio State and his doctorate from Missouri.

Salter left within a year to take a high post with the U.S. Department of Agriculture, and Baver was elevated to take his place as director of research. Baver then brought in Dr. Ralph Cummings from Cornell University as head of agronomy and Dr. A. O. Shaw from Kansas State University in animal science, which included dairying, animal husbandry, dairy processing, and animal nutrition. Baver and Shaw visited the Swannanoa station often during the next three years, and Shaw gave Colvard several special assignments that normally would have been handled by researchers in Raleigh. One experiment was to determine the effect of hormone stimulus on the production of milk in dairy cattle. Another was to see how well swine would do with a primary diet of wheat, which was plentiful and cheap at the time, rather than corn. "They did just as well or a little better on wheat," Colvard recalled.

It was during this time that Colvard again showed that he had excellent, if serendipitous, timing. His old high school vocational agriculture teacher, William LaRue, by 1940 had become associate editor of *Progressive Farmer* magazine in Raleigh. Colvard read an editorial in the magazine, written by editor Clarence Poe, lamenting the fact that no U.S. Secretary of Agriculture had ever been chosen from the South. In response, Colvard wrote the letter pointing out that the region lagged behind the North and Midwest because no southern university offered a doctorate degree in agricultural specialties. "This opinion is based on my own experience in trying to find a school in the South where graduate work might be pursued beyond a Master's Degree in the fields of dairying or animal husbandry," Colvard wrote. His letter found favor from Poe, who undoubtedly shared it with Graham, LaRue, and leaders at NC State.

Poe was more than just a magazine editor and publisher. He was part of the most powerful group of political and business figures in the state at the time. He was well connected with Frank Graham and the state's commissioner of agriculture, W. Kerr Scott, who later would become governor and then a U.S. senator. Scott, a member of the second generation to be connected with improving North Carolina's agriculture, appointed Graham to the U.S. Senate in March 1949 when Senator Melville Broughton died in office. In 1950, Graham lost the seat to Willis Smith in a hard-fought election marked with race-baiting overtones.

Poe also was a member of the board of trustees of the consolidated university and chairman of its agriculture committee, a powerful position at the time. As such, he was able to direct monies into North Carolina State College. He was extremely interested in replacing the cotton and tobacco row-cropping system with what he called two-armed farming, meaning a mixture of cash crops with livestock and poultry. He had also been writing about more attention to soil conservation.

Colvard also was able to forge an important early connection with another powerful North Carolina personality, Dr. Howard Odum, an influential professor and social scientist in Chapel Hill and a close friend and adviser to Graham and Scott. Odum and Colvard met because Odum was a hobby breeder of Jersey cattle and president of the North Carolina Jersey Cattle Club and Colvard was the club's secretary.

Although Colvard was exempt from military service because he was the father of two children by this time (daughters Carol, born November 11, 1940, and Mary Lynda, born September 12, 1942), he applied for a commission in the Navy, but was turned down because his eyesight was below standard. Meanwhile, as World War II accelerated, the Army commandeered the Swannanoa station in 1942 as the site of a new 1,520-bed casualty hospital, and Colvard was put to work searching for locations of two new agricultural experiment stations. His search resulted in the state buying a site at Laurel Springs in February 1944 and one in Waynesville in May 1944. Later that year, he and his family moved to a rented apartment in Waynesville and he frequently traveled the 150 miles to Laurel Springs supervising the construction and operation of both stations.

In July 1944, Shaw resigned as director of NC State's animal science department to become superintendent of Coble Dairy Farms in Lexington, North Carolina. Baver replaced him with Dr. James H. Hilton of the dairy department at Purdue University in West Lafayette, Indiana. It was to be another fateful turn of events for Colvard. A native of Catawba County, North Carolina, Hilton had graduated from Iowa State College in 1922 and gone on to receive a master's at the University of Wisconsin and a Ph.D. from Purdue University in 1945. He had become an expert in the nutritive value of soybeans and the vitamin needs of dairy cattle. He had been assistant chief of dairy husbandry at Purdue and resigned to go to NC State as chief of animal sciences. He and Colvard had established an immediate rapport when Hilton visited Colvard at the experimental station in Swannanoa. "Hilton was my mentor," Colvard recalled. "My confidence in him was implicit and I knew I could rely upon his guidance."

With Hilton's arrival at NC State, Colvard was soon to be plucked from the relative obscurity of the mountains and put on the fast track to succeed in the rapid development of NC State as a national leader in agricultural academics. Instead of a nonentity he became a known entity. Other young, dynamic leaders were also being recruited as part of Graham and Baver's plan. They were being brought in from strong agricultural programs at universities in Iowa, Missouri, Indiana, Michigan, Maryland, New York, and other states.

Hilton and Baver, who had been named dean of agriculture in 1943, asked Colvard if he would be interested in studying toward a doctorate degree at Purdue University and then returning to NC State to be head of the dairy section of the Department of Animal Industry. "In many respects this was the opportunity of a lifetime for me," Colvard wrote in his autobiography. "They put together a plan that conformed to both their interests and what they believed to be mine." He told them he was interested, but had to find a way to support his family while he was in school. Hilton and Baver, along with sponsorship from Frank Porter Graham and Howard Odum, sought a fellowship for him from the General Education Board in New York, created by the Rockefeller Foundation in 1902 to assist educational efforts across the South. "He knows how to organize and conduct research," Baver said in his sponsoring letter of July 2, 1945. "He has the confidence of the farmers. He has enthusiasm, ability, and personality. He is interested in entering Purdue University to obtain his doctorate with considerable emphasis on the economic and sociological aspects of dairying."

Although Colvard never did find out what the "sociological aspects of dairying" were, the General Education Board approved a grant for him of $2,160 for a year, plus $318 for tuition and fees. Colvard then resigned from his state job effective January 31, 1946, giving up his annual salary of $3,636. (Future North Carolina commissioner of agriculture Jim Graham succeeded him as manager of the Laurel Springs operation.) In his letter of resignation, dated October 31, 1945, Colvard said his opportunity to study at Purdue and return to NC State "offers a field of great service to the livestock industry of North Carolina."

Colvard planned to enroll for Purdue's spring semester, which was to begin on March 1. He and Martha decided she and the two girls should stay at her parents' home in Osawatomie, Kansas, until he could get settled at Purdue and find a suitable house or apartment.

Colvard buckled down to studying animal sciences and economics.

His main assignment while at Purdue was to study subjects that would help the discovery of new uses of land in the South that had formerly been used for cotton crops. "The cotton crop had been taken away largely by the boll weevil, but also by tenants moving away," he recalled. "We were trying to find a way of using this land that had been vacated by the disappearance of the cotton crop, and one of the avenues being pursued at NC State was to increase the development of livestock. This would be done by finding pastures and feed crops that could be grown on the severely eroded and fertility-depleted soil."

After finishing his courses in agriculture economics and animal science, Colvard was assigned a thesis titled "The Future of the Livestock Industry in the Southeastern States." His research was financed by a grant from Swift & Company, a major meat processor in the United States. Colvard completed his course work in February 1947 and reported to his new job in Raleigh. His salary would be $5,500 per year.

NC State was certainly one of the most exciting and advantageous places in the nation to be in the late 1940s if you were an ambitious agricultural academic. Colvard's old acquaintance W. Kerr Scott had been elected governor in 1948, after having served as state agriculture commissioner for twelve years, and was leaning hard on the legislature for funds to upgrade NC State. The Rockefeller Foundation was pouring money into it, and it was gaining support from other foundations as well as the U.S. Department of Agriculture.

Colvard was soon a busy young man. In addition to his academic duties, he also would have to find time to finish his thesis. "My research required collecting extensive data, studying numerous reports, and of time-consuming travel to various parts of the southeastern states," Colvard recalled. One of those states was Mississippi, where he visited Mississippi State College in Starkville.

Part of Colvard's research into finding new feed crops that could be grown on former cotton-producing land involved experiments at NC State. "When I finished my course work at Purdue and went to NC State, I found some very good agronomists who were waiting for me." Colvard immediately began evaluating the nutritive value of different experimental crops NC State was growing on a former prison farm near the campus. "One of the principal studies was on a tall fescue grass known as Kentucky 31," he recalled. "We planted Kentucky 31 with ladino clover, orchard grass and some other grasses and measured the nutritive value of them. I was handling the animal-science side of it and others were handling the agronomics, soil fertility and so on." Colvard was in charge of choosing which types of dairy and beef cattle to place on various plots of grass, and then he would keep meticulous records of their weight gains and milk production relating to the grasses they consumed. Colvard had just bought a new home and asked his agronomist colleague, Dr. Roy Lovvorn, what kind of grass would be best for soil in his yard. "He said, 'Why don't you put tall fescue on it?' I did and that's the first fescue lawn I ever saw. Pretty soon it was on lawns all over the state. It was on pastures. It was on roadsides. It was on cemeteries."

Colvard had limited undergraduate teaching duties, but he lectured on artificial insemination of cattle to some undergraduate classes, graduate seminars, and short courses. "My energies were concentrated on the research program, organization of the dairy husbandry section, and initiation of graduate studies." He was particularly keen on upgrading State's program to be able to provide doctorates. Prior to 1944, NC State was not permitted to grant Ph.D.s.

Colvard soon discovered that he had stepped into the middle of a department that was going through extreme transition. Old hands were retiring and new ones like himself were being brought on board in an effort to put NC State among the forefront of agricultural teaching and research universities nationwide, just as Frank Porter Graham had directed. It was a dizzying pace as Baver pushed hard for progress. But Baver resigned in 1948 to take a job as director of research for the Hawaiian Sugar Planters Association, and Dr. James Hilton was named to succeed him. Colvard, who was only thirty-five and still had not submitted his dissertation, was appointed to succeed Hilton. "Although this was unexpected and, even to me, seemed somewhat premature, it was nevertheless challenging," he wrote.

Colvard believed that he had some influence in the positive change in direction at NC State. But he wrote in his autobiography, "Whether or not I had any influence on the changes in program emphasis of the School of Agriculture, I was fortunate to be 'sitting on the doorsteps' when new leaders were recruited and to be chosen to participate in the new directions that were emerging."

Howard Odum wrote to the Rockefeller Foundation after Colvard had been at NC State a year: "Colvard made good at Purdue and has done an exceptionally fine piece of work here at the University of North Carolina. This is an excellent example of how much this sort of thing is worth to a young man who would always have done well but would have lacked the final attainments to go to the top unless he had been encouraged to go on." Colvard continued to work hard during 1948 and 1949 recruiting top agriculture researchers as his budget would allow. Finally he was able to finish his dissertation and received his Ph.D. from Purdue on June 18, 1950.

The only memorable experience Colvard encountered regarding racial matters occurred the next year. As chairman of the NC State Department of Animal Industry, he organized the first statewide dairy farmers conference and sent invitations out to all Grade A dairy farmers in the state, without a thought as to whether some would be black. The luncheon was held in the college cafeteria, where blacks usually disappeared to eat elsewhere and returned for the speeches. This time the black dairy farmers stayed, were served, and the affair went off without a hitch. "My wife and I had never considered ourselves zealous crusaders for integration, but we had on many occasions supported equal opportunities and justice for all races," Colvard wrote in *Mixed Emotions*, his book about his experiences at Mississippi State.

Things were going along swimmingly at NC State for Colvard until 1952 when Chancellor John Harrelson retired and Colvard's mentor, James Hilton, resigned as dean to become president of Iowa State University at Ames. "This promptly injected my name into the picture as one of the persons most likely to succeed him (Hilton)," Colvard wrote in *Education Was My Ticket*. "My response was that I was not applying for the position." After several months in limbo as the college's governing board searched for a new chancellor, Colvard was named dean, effective July 1, 1953. "Needless to say I was somewhat awed but very tired and relieved," he noted. His old friend, Kerr Scott, who had served as governor from 1948 to 1952 and was in between stints of public service while working his farm at Haw River, wrote him a short note: "Dear Colvard, Are you glad you didn't surrender at Swannanoa? Congratulations, Sincerely, W. Kerr Scott."

The succeeding years were busy for the new dean with conferences, committee appointments, and the creation of new departments, including one for genetics. Colvard recommended and received approval of a record number of William Neal Reynolds Distinguished Professor appointments to members of his faculty. He was also credited with helping to bring the "agribusiness" concept to North Carolina agriculture.

An inveterate joiner, Colvard began attending national professional meetings, which exposed him to agricultural leaders from all across the country. He was active in national organizations, including the American Dairy Science Association, the American Society of Animal Production, and the American Farm Economics Association. In Raleigh, he was a key leader in the Rotary Club and his church. Along the way he was named *Progressive Farmer's* North Carolina Man of the Year in 1954 in agriculture. The accompanying story credited him, among other accomplishments, with making the college's tobacco research program "the most effective in the world." Colvard also was named to the board of directors of the Federal Reserve Bank of Richmond. The U.S. Chamber of Commerce put him on the panel to choose the outstanding young farmers of America. In 1958 U.S. Secretary of Agriculture Ezra Taft Benson named him to chair a national study committee on soil and water conservation.

NC State had been asked to provide technical assistance to Peru, and Colvard supervised the establishment of the program in Lima, sponsored by the U.S. and Peruvian governments. NC State School of Agriculture director of research Ralph Cummings moved to Lima in 1955 as the NC State head of the program, which was designed primarily to increase food production. Colvard visited there in 1955 and 1958 to confer with Cummings on the program. He was also named to a key committee in the National Association of State Universities and Land-Grant Colleges and the agricultural advisory committee of the W. K. Kellogg Foundation in Battle Creek, Michigan.

For recreation, he and Martha learned to play golf, and they would travel south from Raleigh to check on the status of a 200-acre pine tree farm they had bought in Richmond County, North Carolina.

All Colvard's travels and activity paid off when he was elected president of the Association of Southern Agricultural Workers. The organization had been formed by the various southern state commissioners of agriculture to bring professionals such as extension directors and experimental farm managers together at regional meetings to discuss common problems. Colvard's service with this organization brought him into contact with leaders from all over the South, including P. O. Davis, director of agricultural extension at Auburn University. Davis would become an important part of Colvard's future.

NC State Chancellor Carey Bostian appointed Colvard as one of three deans to serve on the committee to plan and develop the Research Triangle Park and the Research Triangle Institute. When Bostian stepped down in 1959 to return to teaching, Colvard's name was one of several put forward to succeed him, although Colvard never applied for the job and tried to get his name removed from consideration. For several months, the governing board considered different candidates, finally settling on Dr. John Caldwell, a native of Mississippi and a graduate of Mississippi State. He would come to Raleigh in August 1959 from the presidency of the University of Arkansas at Fayetteville. Colvard was pleased with Caldwell's appointment at NC State.

He noted that he was not too disappointed in not being chosen NC State chancellor. "My family and I felt a great sense of relief," Colvard wrote. "Martha and the children were never interested in the possibility of my becoming involved." By this time, he had three children, since Dean Wallace Colvard, Jr., was born on November 13, 1948, in Raleigh.

In September 1959, Colvard was courted by Ohio State University in Columbus to become its dean of agriculture, but after visiting there he turned it down. "At this juncture in my career, I had resolved that my job at North Carolina State College was more rewarding to me than any similar position in the United States," he noted. "Any uncertainties which may have grown out of the North Carolina State College chancellor selection process had been more than offset by widespread expressions of support and confidence."

Despite the problems, it had been a satisfying time for Colvard. He had worked with Frank Porter Graham and two of his successors, Gordon Gray and Bill Friday. He had forged positive relationships with W. Kerr Scott, who had been elected to the U.S. Senate in 1954, as well as Governor Luther Hodges, and he had helped groom several students who became leaders of the state in later years. These included Scott's son, Robert, who later became a governor, James B. Hunt, later governor for an astounding sixteen years, Eddie Knox, who became mayor of Charlotte, and Phil Carlton, later a prominent lawyer and judge. "I was promoted too soon, but I handled it, I think, reasonably well," Colvard said of his years at NC State.

One of his final acts was to secure the largest grant in NC State's history, $759,800 from the Kellogg Foundation to establish an agriculture policy institute in Raleigh. "What it did was to bring together people who were making decisions on agricultural policy for government expenditures in areas such as soil conservation, water resource control," Colvard recalled. The grant financed seminars and workshops among agricultural, political, and educational leaders throughout the South, as well as the development of courses at NC State and expanded research into the future of southern agriculture.

But just six months after turning down the job at Ohio State, Colvard received another offer—one he decided to accept because it would give him a chance to put his theories about running a large university into action.

Dr. Gordon Ross (left) married Martha Lampkin and Dean Colvard in Berea
College's Danforth Chapel, July 7, 1939.

Where Colvard grew up in Ashe County, N.C.

Colvard (left) and Ralph Cummings, Director of Research, examine a tall fescue pasture experiment at NC State, 1948.

W. Kerr Scott, Commissioner of Agriculture, and Jersey bull, Oxfordia Lad of Morrocraft, at Swannanoa Research Station, 1938.

Dean Colvard in his first long pants, visiting relatives in Wilkes County, 1927.

The Wiley P. Colvard family in 1948. Seated, left to right: Audrey, Wiley, Mary, Carol Wade. Standing: Charles Deward, Ruby, Arleine, Mabel, Dean.

Dean and his son, Wallace, ride Daisy, the gentle mare, on Colvard Farm in Ashe County, 1950.

Wiley P. and Mary Shepherd Colvard, 1948.

2

TESTING THE
"UNWRITTEN LAW"

Some lights were still on in the big old house that served as the president's residence at Mississippi State University. The president was up late on this chilly February night in 1963 because he was wrestling with an unusual decision, one that he knew would raise hell and put his job in jeopardy. The sports world on the national scene would call him a hero, but many in Mississippi and other Deep South states would brand him a traitor.

It was ironic, Dean W. Colvard thought, that, after nearly three years of excellent progress as the university's first outsider president in history, athletics, not academics, would create his first real crisis.

At a regional alumni meeting soon after his arrival, he had responded to a question about his position on athletics by saying that he expected to be president of the whole university, including athletics. He felt that after more than two years his support should be strong enough to allow him to face his first real test as president, one that would pit him against the state's political leadership.

The fulcrum point had come earlier that February night when the outstanding MSU basketball team, ranked seventh in the nation, had beaten Tulane University and clinched its third Southeastern Conference championship in a row. Better than vaunted Kentucky. Better than MSU's hated rival Ole Miss. As champions, MSU automatically would be invited to represent the conference at the National Collegiate Athletic Association Midwest Regional Tournament, along with three other conference teams.

But despite the MSU team's success, it appeared the Maroon Bulldogs —with four seniors on the starting five—would have to stay home for the third year in a row. Last year rival Kentucky had gone in their place and the year before it was Georgia Tech. Unless President Colvard broke with tradition, the university again would turn down the invitation to compete in the prestigious national tourney.

The problem was Mississippi's so-called unwritten law. It prevented teams from Mississippi's state-supported colleges and universities from playing any integrated team, and it had already been reported that the SEC champion would be playing a team that had four black players on the starting five.

No one in authority expected this year to be any different in Mississippi, and the press was reporting that chances of MSU going to play in the tournament at East Lansing, Michigan, were slim. "State's Coach Still Hopeful, but NCAA Picture Dim," reported the Memphis *Commercial-Appeal* the morning after the Tulane victory, and the story quoted the chairman of the athletics committee of Mississippi's governing board of trustees as saying his committee would vote against any MSU trip.

This was going to be a difficult decision for the MSU president, despite the fact that coach and team members had said they wanted to go ahead, and the student body and alumni were clamoring for the event. Colvard was the lone, last hope because all others who could have authorized the change—the governor, the legislature, and the university's governing board—had either denied such a possibility or passed the buck. Governor Ross Barnett, internationally known for his segregationist stand at Ole Miss six months earlier, was on record against an MSU trip. Leading segregationist legislators had threatened budget cuts or worse as reprisal if anyone dared violate the infamous unwritten law. State representative Walter Hester told the press, "It is no safer to mix with Negroes on the ball courts than in the classroom. Mississippi State has capitulated and is willing for Negroes to move into that school en masse." And the chairman of the governing state Board of Trustees of Institutions of Higher Learning said it was not going to act, leaving such a decision up to Colvard.

Any hopes that the governing board would take the initiative and order the team to represent the SEC in the NCAA playoffs were dashed when the board met that February in Jackson and decided not to decide. "The Board was not inclined to exercise any initiative in this matter," Colvard wrote in his diary that February night at his desk in the corner of the living room of the President's House. "This, of course, would have me clearly taking the brunt of public reaction but it was speculated that the Board would be less likely to censure me than to grant permission for the team to go." (Colvard not only kept a detailed diary, but also wrote a book, *Mixed Emotions*, about his experiences at MSU.)

His decision could destroy his future usefulness to MSU, Colvard told his wife, Martha, but together, with his associates' support, they decided it was the right time and the right thing to do. He told her to expect some angry telephone calls when he was not home, and the campus police chief put a twenty-four-hour watch on the house. It was no casual act. The Voter Education Project had just released a report that listed sixty-four acts of violence and intimidation against blacks in Mississippi since January 1961. Martha remained calm and kept the household running as usual, even though she was alone sometimes in the house. She continued her extensive duties as "the quintessential college president's wife," as one observer noted, hosting events for faculty and visiting dignitaries.

Colvard was taking a risk, but it was a calculated one. In his meticulous style, he had done careful research and discovered that there was no written policy or law restricting him from approving post-tournament play, black opponents or not. There was only the mysterious unwritten law. He knew he was the team's last hope, and he knew there was still a very real possibility that his act could be rescinded. The governing board could call a special meeting and, if a simple majority of its members present caved in to pressure from segregationist forces, Colvard's decision could be reversed. If that happened, Colvard knew it would mean the end of his presidency. All his hard work since he had become MSU's chief executive on July 1, 1960, all the receptions in the big house, the reorganizing, lobbying, building, hustling support from legislators, alumni, and the state's business leaders, all the trips and speeches to civic clubs and all types of other organizations all over the state would be put in serious jeopardy.

But again Colvard had done his homework. He and his staff had estimated how each member of the thirteen-person board would vote and concluded that if they were forced to vote the outcome would be uncertain. (Seven votes were needed; although the board had thirteen members, only twelve were eligible to vote, since one could vote only on matters pertaining to Ole Miss.) Even at this point Colvard was still taking a risk because he knew that men had changed their minds many times before when subjected to vicious race-baiting.

And little did he know that another completely unexpected challenge would lie ahead, one that would send him hurrying out of town to avoid legal action and one that would require a complex cloak-and-dagger episode before the team could be sent on its way.

Mississippi's seeming obsession about racial mixing was more than a hypothetical to Colvard. He knew that just a hundred miles to the north in Oxford, federal troops still occupied the campus at Ole Miss, six months after riots erupted there during the integration of the university. (The troops would leave only when the lone black student, James Meredith, graduated in August 1963.) Two people had been killed and dozens injured. The governor who had led the defiance, Ross Barnett, was still in office in February of 1963, and the membership of the board of trustees, who had acceded its power to the governor in the crisis, had remained the same.

Barnett had burst onto the scene in May 1955 by winning a judgment in New York requiring the *Communist Daily Worker* newspaper to apologize to one of his clients in Laurel, Mississippi, for libelous statements about her insinuating that she had enticed a Negro man who was eventually charged with rape and convicted. A photograph of Barnett reading the apology appeared in several Mississippi papers. His stump speech usually included the lines, "When agitators come into our midst to sow seeds of discord in an effort to destroy our great traditions and way of life, we will stand as firm as the old famed Rock of Gibraltar. We will convince the world that we are capable and determined to govern our own internal affairs." In one of his "Roll with Ross" campaign advertisements, he said, "Because of my long experience in legal procedure, I can raise more technical points than the Supreme Court can consider in the next hundred years! As long as Ross Barnett is governor, Mississippi will have segregated schools."

During the Ole Miss uproar, Colvard considered making a public statement calling for adherence to federal law. But he felt that he would have had to resign and decided he was needed more at MSU than any other place. He knew then that it would be only a matter of time before he was confronted with other decisions involving racial matters. "The atmosphere of deep hate and vindictiveness which prevails so widely in Mississippi is far from inspiring," he wrote in his diary at the time. "I cannot stay in it indefinitely. However I must try to keep the university conscious of its great responsibility in the training of the young people of Mississippi and in the total development of the state." Colvard already had been confronted in the spring of 1962 by a state legislator who urged him to cancel a commencement speaker known for his moderate stance on racial matters. "When I did not weaken in my commitment," Colvard wrote, "he then asked me a very blunt and scurrilous question: 'Are you a nigger lover or a nigger hater?' I hung up!"

Although he thought the team should have gone on to the NCAA championship competition after winning the SEC crown in 1961 and 1962, Colvard remained quiet because he wanted to build a solid wall of support before beginning to challenge things. No one, not the student body, not the alumni, had asked him to rule against the unwritten law. And Colvard, during his first two years, was busy reorganizing the university administration and visiting alumni leaders and groups around the state.

But by the time the team had won its third straight championship there was a burgeoning clamor for change. Colvard had never played high school or college basketball, concentrating instead on baseball, but he respected and admired skilled athletes, and he felt it was increasingly embarrassing and grossly unfair to deny the team its chance for glory for the third straight time. The student body also began to protest, and two hundred students marched on Colvard's house the night of the Tulane victory. Telephone calls, telegrams, and letters from alumni started pouring in favoring the trip. Colvard's businessman friend, Owen Cooper of Yazoo City, joined the fray, delivering a favorable petition in person; it included the names of prominent business leaders and famous country comedian Jerry Clower, who had once worked for Cooper. The pressures were moving in the direction the president from out-of-state would like to move.

In the SEC's Birmingham headquarters, Commissioner Bernie Moore, probably expecting an MSU withdrawal again, turned up the pressure. Two days after the Tulane victory, Moore told MSU it must accept the NCAA invitation within four more days or the honor would go to second-place finisher Georgia Tech. By this time, Colvard had made up his mind. In discussions with his chief assistant, Dr. Ted Martin, he said, "This is it." He made a few phone calls to key people and then called MSU athletic director Wade Walker and Coach James "Babe" McCarthy into his office to inform them. McCarthy assured him the team members would behave like gentlemen on the trip to Michigan and said, "I admire your heart." All Colvard could say was, "I'm for you and the boys. Go ahead and win." After McCarthy and Walker had left, Colvard noted in his diary, "I went into my washroom and lost a few tears, for what reason I am not sure."

McCarthy had spoken out publicly in favor of the NCAA trip after the 78-67 Tulane victory in New Orleans. "It makes me sick when I have to tell friends I don't think we'll get a chance to go," McCarthy told the *Starkville News* in a postgame interview. "These boys have won three titles in a row, and I don't see why they should have to pack their uniforms Saturday night and let an Alabama or Georgia team represent the SEC when these folks have the same problems we have. To the man, my boys want to go to that tournament. I have said my piece. That is all I can say." When a Memphis *Commercial-Appeal* reporter had asked Colvard on February 12 whether the team would go if it won the SEC title, he replied, "I wouldn't want to comment on this right now." Later that night after the Tulane victory Colvard called his pastor, Robert Walkup of Starkville's First Presbyterian Church, to tell him about his decision, and they had a prayer together.

The next night Colvard went to Meridian to speak at a special dinner honoring Johnny Baker, MSU's All-American football player. "Gov. Barnett was there," Colvard noted in his diary. "Many people were telling him to let our boys play in the tournament. I did not talk with him beyond greetings and casual exchange—very friendly—as he has always been to me."

Colvard had called Senator John Stennis in Washington to tell him of his decision in advance of the announcement. Stennis, who was chairman of the powerful Appropriations Committee, told him that he had made the right decision, that he was behind him all the way, but that he couldn't come out publicly and say so because he was afraid Barnett would use any sign of racial wavering in an attempt to defeat him in the next election. "I never held that against Stennis because that was reality," Colvard said. "I had no doubt at all that Barnett would use whatever tool he could play and I did not want to see him beat John Stennis. Stennis was the strongest supporter I had in Mississippi, and the last thing I wanted him to do was sacrifice himself for me."

Colvard decided to announce his decision in conjunction with MSU's last game of the season against Ole Miss that Saturday night, March 2, at Oxford. Win or lose, the Maroons already had the SEC championship wrapped up, but it was always sweet to defeat the Rebels.

More pressure came when it was learned that the president of state-supported Delta State College that day had turned down the NCAA's bid to play in the small-college tournament rather than violate the unwritten rule.

But Colvard's timing was excellent. He had his statement released at 7:45 P.M., fifteen minutes before the MSU Maroons took the floor against Ole Miss. "This statement is the result of my best effort to do my duty, as I see it, toward the students and faculty of Mississippi State University, its alumni and friends, and the people of Mississippi," Colvard began. "Whatever shortcomings it reveals are failures in capacity or judgment. They may not rightly be ascribed to failure in desire to do the right thing." He said that the so-called unwritten law was obscure and possibly did not even exist. He also said he had received favorable recommendations from alumni, the university's athletic director, its athletics committee, and a petition signed by 3,000 students seeking the post-season trip.

"In answer to this manifestation of interest and in the light of my best judgment, it is my conclusion that as responsible and responsive members of the academic community and of the Southeastern Conference we have no choice other than to go. Accordingly, as President of Mississippi State University I have decided that unless hindered by competent authority I shall send our basketball team to the NCAA competition." (Colvard said later that he inserted the phrase "unless hindered by competent authority" not as a challenge to the governing board, but as evidence that he recognized the board's ultimate authority.) He continued that he had made his decision freely and independently. "As one who has lived in the midst of Mississippians for less than three years, I am cognizant of the hazard of this action and am fully reconciled to the possible consequences of it upon my professional career."

MSU's players will represent the state well, he said. "My conviction is that the well-trained young people of Mississippi can compete on a favorable basis, athletically and intellectually, with the best in other parts of the country and that our champions are entitled to the opportunity to compete. I am further convinced that the spirit of fair play on the part of all concerned at the scene of the NCAA playoffs will transcend whatever prejudice or bias may obtain and transmute all participants into their essential roles as champions competing for the crown." He closed with, "My feelings and my faith are that the reception of our team, in recognition of their conduct and spirit, will serve

to allay the concern of those who question the wisdom of the participation. My hope for the team is an enjoyable time, good, clean competition, and victory."

(When E. R. Jobe, executive secretary of the board of trustees, had
been advised by telephone that Colvard's statement included the information that he as well as the board chairman and athletic committee chairman had been told of the MSU president's decision in advance,
Jobe immediately had contacted the remaining board members. This
led to a leak of the information to many members of the state legislature who were opposed to the decision.)

The fired-up team took a 75-72 victory against their archrivals in
Oxford, ending the season with a 21-5 record. Colvard was not there to
watch the triumph. He and his wife and son, Wallace, were in the Peabody Hotel in Memphis. "We felt somewhat like fugitives hiding away,"
Colvard wrote in his diary, "but we knew that nothing could be changed
or accomplished by further conversations." He was unable to get the
game on the radio in his room at the Peabody, so he telephoned his
secretary, Bettye Douglas, in Starkville, and she placed the receiver by
her radio so Colvard could listen. The connection kept fading in and
out, and he missed the announcement of his decision and the following roar of the crowd. The next day Martha and Wallace went back to
Starkville while Colvard went on to New York City, where he was to
confer with Rockefeller Foundation officials about possible funding
for one of MSU's projects.

Meanwhile, the telephone at the president's house began to ring as
angry protestors threatened violence against Colvard, and a few supporters registered their opinions.

An anonymous threat came in the form of a mimeographed sheet of
paper distributed around town from a group calling itself Sons of Mis-
sissippi, Rebel Underground. Addressed to "Citizens of Mississippi," the
flyer began, "IT IS NOW OR NEVER IF WE ARE TO PRESERVE OUR FREE-
DOM WHICH LEFTWINGERS ARE TRYING TO DESTROY AT MSU. NEVER BE-
FORE IN THE HISTORY OF OUR GREAT STATE HAS A PRESIDENT, ACTING
UNDER THE DIRECTION OF THE NAACP, SOUGHT TO DESTROY OUR CHER-
ISHED WAY OF LIFE AS COMRADE COLVARD WITH HIS PUPPET MCCARTHY
IS TRYING.

"IT WOULD BE GREAT TO HAVE OUR BASKETBALL TEAM KNOWN AS
NATIONAL CHAMPIONS, BUT WHAT A PRICE WE WOULD HAVE TO PAY.
ONLY A FOOL STAYS TO PICK UP PIECES OF GOLD KNOWING THAT A
WALL IS FALLING ON HIM. THE PRICE WE WILL HAVE TO PAY FOR OUR

WAY OF LIFE IS GREAT AND IF WE MISS JUST ONE PAYMENT ALL WILL BE LOST. MCCARTHY MUST NOT BE ALLOWED TO TAKE OUR BASKETBALL TEAM UP NORTH AND DESTROY THE THING MOST DEAR TO OUR FORE-FATHERS.

"BUT COMRADE COLVARD IS NOT JUST STOPPING WITH BASKETBALL AND THE OTHER SPORTS. HE ALONG WITH THE INFAMOUS AAUP [American Association of University Professors] HAS MAPPED OUT STRATEGY FOR THE COMPLETE INTERGRATION OF OUR GREAT UNIVERSITY. MERE WORDS WILL NOT STOP THIS OBSESSED DRIVE. ACTION IS NEEDED, CITIZENS OF MISSISSIPPI. STAND UP AND BE COUNTED NOW OR FOREVER SUFFER THE CONSEQUENCES."

Secretly the Soverignty Commission stepped up its surveillance of Colvard. Somebody entered the first newspaper clipping, dated March 4, with a headline, "Little Opposition Heard to State's NCAA Entry," in Colvard's file at the commission's headquarters in Jackson. But this entry wasn't the first. The commission had been keeping tabs on Colvard at least since January 1961, just six months after he became president of Mississippi State.

The first entry was a curious one, a roster of the state's agricultural extension workers—black and white—across the state with Colvard's name at the top as their superior. The list was dated October 21, 1960, and entered into the commission files the following January 21. Other entries consisted of newspaper clippings about the Mississippi State basketball team going to play in the NCAA regionals in March 1963. There are no clues as to why the clippings were inserted into the files. Only the initials J. D. appear at the end of one, and none of the commission's three investigators had those initials. None of the other staff members listed in Erle Johnston's book, *Mississippi's Defiant Years*, including one Naomi Scrivner, "a lady who read textbooks and other material to see if they were 'questionable,'" had those initials either. When the files were finally opened to the public thirty-eight years later, there was no accompanying data to explain why such records were being kept on Colvard. Years later Colvard could not recall being involved with anyone with the initials of J. D. during that time period who would have had a reason to spy upon him.

Although Erle Johnston, who was director of the Sovereignty Commission in 1963, went to his grave before explaining who J. D. was, it was clear that the commission had done its job for thirteen years—from 1956 to 1973—to investigate anyone "with any stain of Communism or involvement with Communist groups or publications, and also any persons or organizations that attempted to violate the state's laws on segregation." It was a wide-reaching mandate from the legislature, and the directors over the years played fast and loose with the surveillance program. "I was awed by my position," Johnston wrote in his autobiography, *Mississippi's Defiant Years.* "I equally was awed with what I could do with it. The bill creating the Sovereignty Commission in 1956 made no mention of segregation. It had authority to issue subpoenas but I never knew of any being issued. . . . As I studied our setup and read the law, about all they [commission investigators] could do was gather information. Some of it would be worthwhile if we could relay it to proper law enforcement authorities about planned events that might be prevented, or at least, be controlled."

Johnston wrote that the agency not only had paid informants, but that "we felt obligated to know what was going on, and what was being planned, among the civil rights activists," although he denied that the commission ever wiretapped any phones or installed any electronic surveillance devices.

In his book he said he used various aliases to make contacts "into civil rights groups and into other areas that I will not reveal." Incredibly, he wrote, "Since we dealt with various detective agencies and depended on their contacts for information, I did not even know the identity of sources. All of them were anonymous and even if I happened to know any names, I promised confidentiality and will honor it in this book."

Johnston's book was published in 1990, eight years before the files would be opened, but he proudly proclaimed, "We acquired voluminous files on identities, movements, and backgrounds of subversive individuals and organizations who joined in the racial movement, sometimes as effective associates but often merely to create turmoil." The agency was decommissioned in 1973, but Johnston probably felt confident that his activities would not be challenged in his lifetime, since the legislature had ordered the files closed in 1977 for fifty years, or until 2027. It took a federal court order to open them for the first time in 1998. In his book Johnston acknowledged, "Many incidents never were written into the files because of the confidentiality and possible embarrassment to leaders of both races." However, he cited several cases where information was gathered on several individuals and secretly passed along to law enforcement agencies or news media in attempts to discredit the individuals.

At least one news reporter, Walter Rubager of the New York Times

News Service, learned of the commission secret files and tactics, and Johnston included part of Rugaber's report in his book without comment. Rugaber wrote, "A secretly prepared official report has disclosed details of a four-year campaign by the Mississippi State Sovereignty Commission to harass and discredit the civil rights movement in the state. Participants in the anti-segregation efforts often were anonymously denounced as Communists. Outsiders interested in helping Negroes were urged to go elsewhere. A network of spies kept local officials informed about the plans of integrationists. The report outlines Mississippi's undercover resistance to racial crusades such as the Freedom Summer of 1964, the political challenge of the Freedom Democratic Party, and the James Meredith March of 1966."

Johnston never denied Rugaber's report, he merely complained that the *New York Times* had misinterpreted the data from a report that he had submitted to Governor Paul Johnson, Jr., in late 1967. Rugaber's charges were borne out in 1998 when the files were finally opened to the public on March 17, 1998. "Dozens of agents and informants were on the commission payroll," the Associated Press reported on the occasion, "ferreting out gossip, tall tales and, sometimes, facts about those involved in the civil rights movement and voter registration drives in Mississippi."

Time magazine writer John Cloud got a look at the files and reported, "Even now, years after the most damning files were almost certainly purged, the records reveal ugly abuses of power. The commission's investigators spied on almost anyone, black or white, who publicly promoted racial equality—most often local civil rights workers but also visiting Yankees. Commission investigators documented the whereabouts, finances and sexual habits of civil rights leaders. They fed some of the information to the targets' employers and the Ku Klux Klan. Untold numbers of people were fired and perhaps even killed after the commission targeted them."

Former Mississippi Governor William Winter of Jackson said that in his opinion there was no question that the Sovereignty Commission was attempting to gather information on Colvard. Years later Colvard recalled, "I was aware of the Sovereignty Commission, of course, but I had no idea that the commission's staff had me under surveillance. It wouldn't have made any difference to me anyway because I was doing what I thought had to be done and what had the approval of more than 3,000 students and various alumni groups."

On that same Monday, March 4, 1963, after Colvard's announcement that MSU was sending the team to East Lansing, the fires of racial conflict were fanned by the announcement that the NAACP had filed suit in Jackson calling upon the federal court to force the public schools to be integrated. Constant critic James Ward, editor of the *Jackson Daily News*, blamed Colvard, although the suit obviously was planned many months before. "Obviously elated over the announcement by D. W. Colvard of Mississippi State University that the Maroons basketball team would indulge in a little integration at the NCAA Tournament in Michigan, the NAACP has filed a suit to force race mixing in the classrooms of Jackson," Ward wrote. "It should be borne in mind that the decision made at Starkville involved more than a Roman lust for another basketball trophy. Athletic fans went nuts and lost their sense of values in the days of Caesar and great was the fall of the empire."

Martha Colvard answered most of the protesting telephone calls she received at the President's House by telling them her husband was at the office, but their son, fifteen-year-old Dean Wallace Colvard, Jr., whom they called Wallace, also answered a few. One from an angry, anonymous woman frightened him. Wallace recalled later, "I said hello and this woman immediately said something like, 'Tell your dad what he's doing is not right. I'm going to take my son out of the university and you had better watch out because there are a lot of people who don't like what he's doing.'" He considered it a threat, but he never told his father about it. "I thought he was busy enough," he said.

Any euphoria over Colvard's Saturday night decision was short-lived. On Monday, five members of the governing board—led by Colvard critic and staunch segregationist M. M. Roberts of Hattiesburg—called for a special meeting to debate the MSU president's action, and on Tuesday the board's chairman, Tom Tubb of West Point, set the meeting for 2:00 P.M. on the following Saturday, March 9, in Jackson. Again, howls of outrage on both sides of the issue erupted. The state's newspapers had a field day, with most editorializing against the trip but more than a few favoring Colvard's decision. The state's largest newspapers, the *Jackson Daily News* and the *Clarion-Ledger*, blistered Colvard's decision. They published the names and addresses of board members in an obvious ploy that they might be contacted and urged to reverse the decision.

The afternoon *Daily News* said, "The glitter of another basketball trophy understandably can blind a rabid basketball fan or over-eager sports writer, but it should not be so dazzling as to prompt grown men of grave responsibility to dash off into an experimental expedition that has been found time and time again to produce sordid results." And the morning *Clarion-Ledger* was even stronger, saying it was "disappointed, disgusted and nauseated to think that Mississippians have weakened to the extent that they will tolerate such a below the belt blow from the head of any college or university." Both papers ran photos of the Loyola team to clearly show that four of the starting five players were black. The Jackson papers never contacted Colvard for a comment, but part-owner Henry Hederman wrote him a letter on March 6 asking him to reverse his decision. Colvard never replied.

The editor of the *Summit Sun*, Mary Cain, tore into Colvard as a carpetbagger. "Dr. Colvard's position concerning athletics reveals a fact he admits: he has been in Mississippi only three years and he just doesn't know our people! If he thinks Mississippians—except for a small number of would-be integrationists—would smile on mixed athletics, well he has another thought coming." Editor Thomas Alewine of the *Rankin County News* in Brandon made it clear he was against the trip. "It could be that some folks get the initials NCAA and NAACP mixed up," he wrote. "To us it's the same difference." *Meridian Star* editor James B. Skewes wrote that Colvard undoubtedly had good intentions. "Nevertheless, his action constitutes a breach of the walls of segregation. Especially in these times we should make no compromise regarding our Southern way of life—we cannot afford to give a single inch. Any concessions in this field will encourage integrationists to be ready for further inroads against segregation. Furthermore, concessions will weaken our own will to resist."

On the favorable side, Hodding Carter, editor of the *Delta Democrat Times* in Greenville, called Colvard's decision a very brave step, writing that "MSU's president is going to come under heavy attack." Carter urged "those who support his stand to let him know it—and to let the State College Board know it too, for the board still has the power to undo Dr. Colvard's action." The *Tupelo Journal*'s editor, Harry Rutherford, wrote: "To the College Board we suggest: Let our boys play. Not only let them play but do your best to send them into the national tournament with the best wishes and the enthusiastic encouragement of the overwhelming majority of the citizens of Mississippi."

An unsigned editorial in the *Madison County Herald* read: "One man, Dr. D. W. Colvard, president of the University, had the courage to discard the 'unwritten law' that has kept other good states from playing for the championship. The present finally caught up with the past. We believe that an overwhelming majority of the people of Mississippi want to see their team play the best this country has. Many may have been afraid to speak out, but are heartily in accord with the decision." Back in North Carolina, the Raleigh *News and Observer* took note of Colvard's decision in a positive light. "This took some courage in view of tradition down there, but it was a sensible move," wrote sports columnist Dick Herbert.

The Mississippi State student newspaper, the *Reflector*, editorialized its support: "Should a dynamic university be led by a man with the intelligence to make a decision on the merits of the case and the guts to back it up? Or, should that university be led by a man, who out of fear for his job, would listen to and be persuaded by the politicians who are usually trying to create votes?" Student columnist Malcolm Balfour called Colvard the new "Mr. State College" and commended his leadership. "The easy way out for Dr. Colvard would have been to keep quiet on the matter, and when asked he could merely reply that the higher authorities had said nothing to him about any change in the 'unwritten law,' therefore State should stay home," Balfour wrote. "Dr. Colvard showed himself to be a brave man, a man worthy of our whole hearted support by his gallant stand. We're very, very proud of our president."

Alumnus E. F. White of Okolona wrote to Colvard, "While 100% of us are opposed to integration, also 100% of us are determined to use our influence to keep the tragedy which befell Ole Miss from occurring at State or any other Mississippi school. After the supreme court decided against us, to try to stop integration would be as futile as trying to dam up the Mississippi River. All that would result in would be to drown in racial hatred and conflict."

The national and international media, including newspapers in France and Japan, played the story as a breakthrough in racial matters in the South. "Miss. State Will Play!" the *Detroit Free Press* headline screamed. The *New York Times* editorialized: "From Mississippi comes an item of college news of no great moment in itself, but, we hope, with overtones of the future. It concerns the state's unwritten law that no 'white' college team shall engage in sports against a team that might include a Negro. Year after year, this self-imposed ordinance has governed sports at Mississippi State. And now the sacred law is broken."

Colvard also picked up support from the faculty senate and a few business leaders, including the Okitbbeha County Chamber of Commerce Board of Directors in Starkville. The board passed a resolution endorsing his decision and commending his outstanding leadership.

Most letters to the editor were not encouraging. Some hinted that sending the team to play an integrated one would be opening the doors to social mixing and eventually mixed blood. Edwin White of Lexington wrote to the *Jackson Daily News:* "For the sake of those who have gone before, for the sake of our women and children, for the sake of those yet to be born, let us prayerfully and conscientiously review this whole matter and decide whether the chance of winning an integrated national basketball tournament is worth the probability of weakening our defenses against racial integration, and inviting more integration efforts against us."

Letter writer Mrs. Orley Hood of Vicksburg put Colvard in with other infiltrators who had become dupes of the Communists trying to take over America. "A study of Communist publications shows that the plot of the international conspirators to conquer the USA hinges on their ability to cause the educators and the clergy to give aid and impetus to their use of the race issue as a means of demoralizing and dividing the people." N. E. Dacus of Tupelo wrote that if Colvard's decision were allowed to stand it would mean the beginning of the end of the white race in America. "If history is still being written 100 years from now, perhaps a visiting scientist may record seeing an American Jungle peopled by a dark brown race of men living in clusters of thatched huts super-imposed upon ruins of brick and steel."

The debate continued hot and heavy as Saturday's board vote approached. At his weekly Wednesday press conference, Governor Barnett made it clear he was against the trip, but he would not order the governing board to reverse Colvard's decision. "The people of Mississippi know that I am a strong believer in and an advocate of segregation in every phase of activity in all of our schools," Barnett said. "Under Section 213A of the Mississippi State constitution, the control of our colleges and universities rests with the Board of Trustees of Higher Learning. Personally, I feel it is not for the best interest of Mississippi State University, the state of Mississippi, or either of the races," Barnett said.

Barnett, a lawyer from Jackson, was the perfect caricature of a Deep South governor, but more cagey than most of his constituents realized. After two previous attempts at being elected governor, he finally won in 1959 on a pledge to keep Mississippi free from integration forever. Barnett became world famous in September 1962 for having publicly faced up against federal troops at Ole Miss, but his image was tainted three months later when *Look* magazine reported that he had made a deal with federal officials that U.S. marshals should draw their guns to make it appear that they were overpowering Barnett's state troopers.

After Colvard's decision in March 1963, Barnett showed again that he was politically savvy by saying he was against the MSU trip, but cannily avoiding further involvement by throwing the matter in the lap of the governing board of colleges and universities. During the Ole Miss uproar, he had taken over higher education control from the same board. Colvard viewed this as the first meaningful hint that the state's adamant stance on segregation might be weakening or beginning to change.

As he waited for Saturday's board meeting to materialize, Colvard again considered stepping down. "I had about made up my mind to resign if the board failed to stand firm," he wrote. "In fact, sometimes I found myself almost wishing I would have enough opposition to give me good reason to resign. But then, our people would express their real concern and almost plead that I take no such drastic action."

The university's security force continued to post around-the-clock sentinels around the president's house, but Colvard never felt that he or his family were in danger. "It was a tense period and I needed some sleeping pills at night," he wrote. "Martha was a very supportive partner in this tense time. I knew we were in a fight and that we had to finish it. I remembered what W. Kerr Scott had said to me about not running away from a little fight." He never carried a weapon during those times, he recalled. "I never expected to get shot. I would not have been surprised if somebody had thrown a burning cross on my lawn or something of that kind, but I never expected anybody to confront me."

Colvard's chief opponent on the state governing board, M. M. Roberts, released a statement to the press: "We have the greatest challenge to our way of life since Reconstruction days, that violence is about to be done to all of Mississippi." He said he would urge the board to reverse Colvard's decision. Roberts, a slim, white-haired man with horn-rimmed eyeglasses who had graduated from MSU, could not be dismissed as a crackpot or weak board member. A skilled lawyer, he was known as a ferocious competitor in and out of the courtroom. A Barnett appointee to the board, he was a near rabid segregationist who was so driven that when he played golf he often played alone, trotting through the course.

The Memphis *Press-Scimitar* threw a scare into Colvard and his supporters on the morning of Wednesday, March 6, when it reported that a highly qualified source said the governing board would reverse Colvard's decision.

When the board gathered in Jackson for the 2:00 P.M. special meeting, four white students picketed out front, and a small delegation of women presented Chairman Tubb with a petition with 130 names protesting Colvard's decision. Colvard and his assistant Martin had checked into a Jackson motel to be available just in case they were needed, and here they waited for word of the outcome of the meeting. Roberts introduced his motion and took to the floor to explain it. "It is a great tragedy that minority pressure groups can cause people to do things they know they shouldn't do," he said. "It looks like we are about to lose our Southern way of life, but we should not voluntarily take on a situation where we are just asking for trouble." Roberts continued to argue for a reversal by the board. "There is no doubt in my mind that he knew he was going against the will of this board," he said. "I resent that. And I think he should resign. He put us on the spot."

Other board members chimed in sparingly and then S. R. Evans of Greenwood called for the vote. Only Roberts, E. Ray Izard of Hazelhurst, and Ira L. "Shine" Morgan of Oxford voted for Roberts's motion. Eight others, including chairman Tubb, voted against it. Still Roberts was not finished; he moved that Colvard be asked to resign, but his motion failed to receive a second. Tally D. Riddell, a competent lawyer and Ole Miss alumnus from Quitman, then moved that the board express confidence in Colvard and this time the vote was 9 to 2 with only Roberts and Izard dissenting. The meeting adjourned at 3:15, but it was not until 3:45 that the board's executive secretary, E. R. Jobe, got around to calling Colvard and Martin at the motel.

"Everybody in Starkville knew the results thirty minutes before we did," Colvard noted in his autobiography. But it soon sank in. "This was good news. We had come out well. I felt relaxed as we drove home from Jackson. There was much happiness on the campus."

Later that Saturday, Barnett, who was in Raleigh, North Carolina, to give a speech, evidently had stuck a political finger in the wind and determined that it was blowing in a new direction. He issued a statement saying the governing board's decision was final and he would honor it. Then he added, "I have great pride in our team and I hope they will win the national championship."

SEC Commissioner Bernie Moore in Birmingham, who had withheld his comments until after the board vote, said, "I would think this would open Southeastern Conference competition in all branches of sports. I think the right decision has been made. Louisiana had an unwritten law of the same kind and broke it to go to the Orange Bowl and the same thing was true with Alabama in the Liberty Bowl." Moore said he was glad the MSU team would make the trip to Michigan. "These are fine boys," he said. "They lost their chance last year and I hope they can make up for it this year, and they will if they just play up to their potential."

That Saturday night after the governing board's endorsement of Colvard's decision, he and Martha were guests at the annual Sigma Chi Sweetheart Ball and received thunderous applause when they were introduced. In his classic, understated manner, Colvard confided to his diary: "The students had watched their president lay his job on the line. Some people thought it was an act of courage. I thought it was simply doing what needed to be done."

Colvard got another boost when the *Durant News* editorialized that perhaps the governing board's decision signaled a "new day" in Mississippi. "Certainly if the vote had been reversed Dr. Colvard would undoubtedly have felt impelled to resign," the editorial said. "This is really not surprising. Mississippians by now are quite used to the extremists who say 'go along with us, or off comes your head.' In the past they have been able to whip practically everyone into line simply by yelling 'nigger' because few people want to be tagged 'integrationist' in this Deep South country. Perhaps the people are weary of this false cry."

But again Colvard and his supporters were soon to discover that their segregrationist foes had hit upon a last-ditch surprise maneuver to attempt to halt the game. Another old nemesis, state senator Billy Mitts of Enterprise, had been at the meeting in Jackson and had announced that he had—unsuccessfully—asked Governor Barnett to call a special session to consider Colvard's decision, which he believed would be reversed by the legislators. Mitts, a former president of the MSU student body, already had tried to introduce a resolution at the legislative session condemning and reversing Colvard's decision. But the resolution died in committee.

Four days after the board vote in Jackson, Colvard had just met at the gym in a huddle with the squad and gave his full support for their victory and was on his way back to his office when MSU's public relations spokesman, Bob Moulder, caught up with him. Moulder told him that he had just had a phone call from an old former coworker at the Jackson newspapers that Mitts had succeeded in getting a judge to issue a temporary injunction to halt the team's trip. The complaint alleged that using state funds for such a trip violated the state law against integration of public facilities. The action asked for a delay until a hearing on the merits of the case could be scheduled.

Moulder said the authorities were on their way from Jackson to Starkville, about 125 miles, to serve papers on Colvard and McCarthy.

Colvard knew that NCAA funds, not the state's, were involved, but that scheduling a hearing would take several days and cause the team to miss its first game on Friday in Michigan. But if the authorities served the papers on him and McCarthy and they ignored the court order, they could be held in contempt and jailed. He soon learned from the college attorney, Buz Walker, that the best thing he and McCarthy could do was avoid being served.

"They were trying to get at me, who had made the decision, and the coach, and stop it," Colvard recalled. "By this time it was about 8:30 and the lawyer said, 'If I were you, I would close the office and not go home.'" Within minutes, Vice President John Bettersworth handed him a packed overnight bag. Bettersworth had called Martha to ask her to pack a bag for her husband. Colvard was supposed to leave for a meeting in Jackson the next morning, but instead he and Bettersworth drove to Birmingham, Alabama, 125 miles to the east, where they spent the night.

McCarthy, athletic director Wade Walker, and his assistant Ralph "Rabbit" Brown had already departed for Nashville, Tennessee, and left assistant coach Jerry Simmons in charge of the team, which was to leave for Michigan the next morning by chartered plane. "Simmons had offers of transportation to remove the team that night, but I asked them to stick to their schedule and use the plane chartered for the next morning," Colvard recalled.

The players had heard about the injunction and nervously waited that night in the dormitory, jumping at every knock on the door or phone call. Senior Leland Mitchell even volunteered to get in his car and drive the five starters to Michigan that night, but he was talked out of it. The next morning, acting on his own, Simmons cautiously sent subs to the airport just in case authorities were there to stop the team. When nothing happened, he and the first string climbed on board for the trip to Michigan, stopping at Nashville to pick up McCarthy, Walker, and Brown.

While the team was on its way to Michigan, Colvard met Martha and Wallace in Chattanooga. They drove to western North Carolina to visit daughter Carol for a few hours before continuing on to Auburn, where Colvard was to deliver a commencement address on Saturday.

They checked into an Auburn motel and then went to dinner with some friends where they were to listen to the MSU-Loyola game on the radio.

Whether they won or lost, Colvard felt good about his decision because Mississippi was being seen in a positive light in contrast to the negative barrage of news that had prevailed so long.

In his diary, Colvard noted: "I really believe that these last two weeks will have significant impact on the leadership of Mississippi—many so-called 'moderate' voices have been heard. As one person who wrote to me put it, maybe we will reach the point that the good people of Mississippi will put their best foot forward all of the time instead of just part of the time."

Thirty-seven years later, Colvard recalled, "Part of my commitment to go to Mississippi State was because I thought it was ready to move."

Somehow the entire episode brought back advice from long ago when he helped his daddy survey land in the North Carolina mountains: "He used to say, 'Don't set your stake down until you're ready.' In other words, make very sure of what you are going to do before you do it, and then do it."

3 THE SLEEPING GIANT

The first time Dean Colvard saw the sleepy campus of Mississippi State University, he was not impressed. When he had gone to Starkville in 1949 during his study for his doctoral dissertation, he thought the buildings looked tired and run-down.

"I met nobody who excited me really, and I came away with the feeling that this wasn't a very vital and active institution," he recalled.

More than ten years would go by before he would have a chance to see the university again, but this time he saw it as a sleeping giant, one that he might be able to wake.

Even then, it was a rather plain-looking collection of brick buildings strung out in a linear fashion along the remains of an old railroad track bed that ran through the heart of the campus. It lacked the charm of an Ole Miss, its rival one hundred miles to the north in Oxford.

Despite the fact that its student body of 4,725 had grown to be the largest in the state, larger than the 3,831 at more historic Ole Miss, founded in 1848, Mississippi State, which had been created thirty years later, still remained the almost forgotten campus, the one with the "cow college" reputation where students arrived straight from the farm. They rang cowbells at football games.

"It was a school in need of visionary leadership," recalled former Mississippi Governor William Winter, who was state tax collector at the time Colvard took over at MSU. "The administration was committed to maintaining the old standards of race relations, the Old South."

MSU had no famous authors like William Faulkner to give it cachet. Its most famous alumni were a politician, U.S. senator John Stennis, who became the epitome of the statesman from the Deep South, and Turner Catledge, a 1922 graduate who became executive editor of the *New York Times* in the early 1950s. (Novelist John Grisham graduated from MSU in 1977, although he did go on to receive his law degree at Ole Miss.)

Located in the heart of an area of cotton fields, cattle farms, and slashpine forest in the east central part of the state close to Alabama, Starkville, with a population of 9,000, the county seat of Okitbbeha County, was no tourist attraction, just a typical small town in Mississippi. But Colvard was not thinking of finding a vacation spot in early 1960 when he was invited to become president of the state's historically agricultural and mechanical institution, the "land-grant" college. He had been beginning to grow weary of the political in-fighting and constant jostling for position and power at NC State, and with the appointment of John Caldwell as chancellor he was wondering if his attachments to previous administrators might be more of a hindrance than a help to the new leader, whom he regarded as a good choice for that position.

So Colvard wanted to find out more when he received a call that February to go to Mississippi for an interview to succeed Mississippi State president Ben Hilbun, who had been in the job since 1953. "Motivated partially by courtesy, partially by curiosity, and partially by a feeling of need for a new challenge, I agreed to go to Jackson and learn more about the situation," Colvard recalled.

The interview was scheduled for March 3, 1960, in Jackson, the state capital where the governing board headquarters was located. Colvard planned to leave the day before, just to be sure he would arrive in plenty of time. But as luck would have it, a rare ice and sleet storm hit much of the South. The airports south of Raleigh were going to be shut down within hours. The easiest thing would have been to cancel, but Colvard was told he could go to Washington instead on a 10:20 A.M. flight and make connections finally into Jackson. Unfortunately, the bad weather forced the plane from Washington to Tampa to halt in Chattanooga, so he had to take a train from there. He finally arrived in Jackson at 8:00 A.M., which meant he had gone more than twenty-four hours without sleep.

As soon as he checked into his hotel, Colvard called the governing board headquarters to say he had arrived, but was running late. He took a quick shower and showed up at his interview a half hour late. The board members were gracious and concerned. They seemed to appreciate the effort he had made to be there.

"My impressions were better than I had expected," Colvard recalled. "They convinced me that the state was improving in income, that the university was ready to move forward, and that this was a challenging opportunity." No one mentioned racial matters nor asked Colvard his feelings about integration. He gently raised the subject himself and was told there was no evidence of any immediate crisis.

At the time of the interview, indeed there was no immediate crisis. No black had applied for admission at an all-white public college or university in Mississippi. Despite the U.S. Supreme Court's rulings, no public school in Mississippi had been integrated. All court challenges had been beaten down on technicalities. Mississippi's leaders had gone on record repeatedly, saying that they would never bow to federal pressure to integrate public facilities. After two previous tries, Ross Barnett had been elected governor on that pledge in the fall of 1959 and had just taken over as chief executive in January 1960.

Colvard believed that attempts at integration at one of Mississippi's white colleges or universities inevitably would follow such actions in North Carolina and a few other southern states. He believed blacks should be entitled to equal treatment and that public officials should abide by federal rulings, but he did not consider himself "sufficiently involved at that time to develop and express a strategy." He was convinced that an integration effort that could not be avoided would come in Mississippi and when it did he knew he would have to take a public stand. "I find myself not running away from the potential race problems as most people think I should," he wrote in his diary on March 24, 1960. "It is a major issue of our time and somehow, while I hope I do not have to be involved in it, I have difficulty in feeling that this should be cause to abandon the idea of going to Mississippi." Later he would recall, "My reasoning was that I am a southerner, of the South. My career is cast in the South, I want it to be in the South, and if the challenge is there I should not run away from it only because it may be tough to handle." Although isolated racial incidents had been occurring all over the South at the time, none had reached the level of those that would follow with bloodshed and violence to vault Mississippi into world headlines time after time. Over the next six years, Mississippi would achieve world fame for incidents involving the riots surrounding the integration of Ole Miss, the killing of three civil rights workers near the town of Philadelphia, and the murder of Medgar Evers, among other events.

Colvard's name had surfaced in the search for a successor to Hilbun, who was retiring. His agricultural organizational activities at NC State had gained considerable national visibility. A Mississippi governing board search committee member, J. N. Lipscomb, who was a former MSU dean of agriculture, had written to P. O. Davis, the director of the agricultural extension service at Auburn University, to ask him about another potential candidate. Davis nixed that man, but wrote back that the committee should take a look at Colvard. "He certainly is worth considering," Davis wrote. "You probably know him. I rate him A-1." He sent Colvard a copy of his letter. Lipscomb, who respected Davis's opinion, made a few telephone inquiries to check Colvard's credentials and then nominated him for consideration as Hilbun's successor. Colvard later found out he was one of twenty-five nominees or applicants.

By mid-March word had leaked out that Colvard was the top candidate for the MSU job, and this elicited telegrams, phone calls, and letters, some from North Carolinians urging him to stay and some from Mississippians urging him to go to Starkville. One letter urging him to remain was from Jesse Helms, who was then executive director of the North Carolina Bankers Association and later a powerful U.S. senator from North Carolina. Helms wrote, "I hope the State of Mississippi will keep its cotton-pickin' hands off the best darned Dean of Agriculture in the U.S. We need you here. On the other hand, I need not mention that I would want you to do what is best for the Colvards. I just hope that the 'best' is for you to stay here."

Representative of the other side was a telegram from Mississippi commissioner of agriculture S. I. Corley: "I urge that you take it [the MSU presidency] and [I] pledge full 100 percent cooperation of State Department of Agriculture. Knowing your leadership is what Mississippi needs."

The MSU search committee flew Colvard and his wife Martha to Starkville on March 23, and Colvard spent the next day touring the campus and interviewing MSU deans. Martha was shown the president's home by Mrs. Hilbun. Although most of the deans were positive about MSU's future, one raised serious questions. "He said the racial situation would close the schools and possibly the university in the very near future, probably 3 or 4 years," Colvard noted in his diary. "(He said) that attitudes were terrible and that I would really have a tough time."Colvard suspected that the dean's comments were influenced by the fact that the dean had been considered and passed over as MSU president, but he realized that the remarks probably were grounded in some truth. Later that day, the governing board officially offered him a four-year contract at $20,000 per year, the same salary as paid the chancellor at Ole Miss. It was a $3,000 raise from Colvard's salary at NC State, and he would receive free housing, utilities, laundry services, and travel allowance.

"None of my colleagues and friends advised me to accept this offer," Colvard wrote in *Mixed Emotions*. "Some strongly advised against going." But Colvard decided he was up for the challenge and accepted MSU's offer. The announcement was made on Sunday, March 27, and he was to take over on July 1. He would become the first non-native Mississippian to become president since MSU had been founded in 1878.

Colvard noted in his diary on March 28 among his reasons for taking the job: "1. Being President is a broader challenge. 2. The Mississippi people gave us an invitation that seemed wholehearted and almost urgent. 3. The personal consideration (salary, etc.) provide considerable incentive. 4. This is the time (my age [forty-six], girls through high school, etc.) if we are to move. 5. My contribution to North Carolina State University could be at its peak." He also wrote, "There is a building job to do in Mississippi and my greatest talent lies in this field. The move is risky—politics, the racial problem, and insufficient finance present very grave problems in Mississippi. We may not be able to handle them. If we don't venture out, we may regret it. We take the chance."

Once the decision was announced, Colvard began to receive letters of support, including one from Chancellor J. D. Williams at the University of Mississippi. "Your decision to join us in Mississippi is a source of encouragement and inspiration to me," Williams wrote. "You and I are 'outsiders.' That fact need not worry you. I have found that such a condition has its advantages." Williams explained that he had come to Ole Miss from the faculty at the University of Kentucky, where he had gone to college. Former Mississippi State president Dr. G. D. Humphrey wrote to congratulate Colvard, but to warn him as well that he would face problems. "You will have your share of problems, too, I am sure, some of which will be normal for a university president and others of which will be unusual," wrote Humphrey, who had become president of the University of Wyoming at Laramie. He said when he became president at MSU in 1934, "The institution had just lost is accreditation as a result of political interference, and my first job was to get sufficient operating funds to build back the prestige which the institution had lost in every field."

With his decision made, Colvard prepared for a month-long trip on April 11 for Thailand as a consultant at the invitation of the U.S. State Department. It was a strenuous but interesting journey, although Martha could not accompany him. She was there to meet him on May 14 in Washington, D.C., where Senator Stennis had arranged a MSU alumni dinner in their honor. They returned on May 15 to Raleigh, where more than a hundred phone calls, telegrams, and letters of congratulations waited. More than three hundred people came to his farewell dinner in Raleigh where he and Martha were presented with a silver punch bowl, twelve cups, a ladle, and a tray. They also were guests of honor at several private dinner parties that followed. Governor Luther Hodges sent him a note saying, "We shall sorely miss you in North Carolina and I want you to know it has been a distinct pleasure to work with you."

"We really hated to leave North Carolina, to leave our friends and associates and to leave Raleigh," Colvard noted in his diary. "On the other hand there was little evidence that those above me, except Bill Friday, had any real desire to see the agricultural programs move ahead." A few lines later he added, "Guess I was a little tired of battling the North Carolina echelon of University and State administration."

Colvard soon received a portent of things to come when a reporter from the Jackson, Mississippi, newspapers called saying there were rumors that he favored integrating the athletic teams in the Southeastern Conference. Colvard deftly sidestepped the question when he told the reporter that he could not make any official statement since he would not be president of Mississippi State until July 1. He continued that he would make no policy statement before that date and, after that time, no statement without first conferring with the governing board. The reporter did not persist and seemed satisfied with Colvard's remarks. The headline the next day in Jackson read: "New President of MSU Will Continue Policies of Board of Trustees," and the story reflected the same.

Finally, with all their goodbyes said in Raleigh, it was time for the Colvards to leave. On June 29 Colvard drove the family's new 1960

Ford station wagon with Martha's African violets, and Martha, with eleven-year-old Wallace, drove the 1957 Buick in a loose caravan to Starkville. They made several stops along the way to visit relatives and friends and arrived in the 97-degree heat of Starkville on the afternoon of Sunday, July 3.

The next day was July 4, celebrated as Independence Day in other states, but in Mississippi equally as well known as the anniversary of the fall of Vicksburg in 1863, during the Civil War. Starkville was involved only because it had been one of the cities Union forces marched through on their way to Baton Rouge in a diversionary attempt to draw Confederate forces away from Vicksburg. The Colvards spent their first night in the President's House that Tuesday, July 5. The rambling, drafty old residence had been built in 1880. Lacking central air conditioning, it required twelve window units running full blast during the hot Mississippi summer and fall. The house needed extensive repairs, which the governing board readily promised. (Eventually the alterations were completed at a cost of $25,000, but the house still had no central air.)

The Colvards were just happy to be at the end of their long journey and into their new home, which they soon learned came complete with a ghost. The morning after their first night there, Floyd Minor, the house's black handyman, asked if founder and Confederate general Stephen Dill Lee had paid them a visit. They said he had not.

When the Colvards arrived in Mississippi, it was still one of the poorest states in the nation—black families had the lowest median income in the nation of only $1,444 per year—and one of the most rural. Overall personal income was only 52.8 percent of the national average. The state also had the country's highest concentration of African Americans, who made up about half of its population of 2 million. Signs designating White and Colored on public restrooms and drinking fountains were still prevalent. In 1960, after Congress passed a voting rights act, the state legislature had enacted a law authorizing the destruction of voter registration records and amended the Mississippi constitution to add "good moral character" as a qualification for voting.

At MSU, Ole Miss, or any one of other mainline colleges, there were no black students, faculty, or administrative staff members. Blacks could not even attend the football games at MSU.

The atmosphere outside the university campus was even more negative toward race relations. On the very first day of his MSU presidency, July 1, 1960, the Jackson newspapers carried a story with the headline "Mississippi Is Only Segregated Bulwark." The story explained, "Mississippi has become the only state that maintains complete segregation in its school system and does not have a suit seeking to change the situation." The article continued by saying that fourteen new laws detailing more segregation had just been adopted by the legislature in Jackson.

The bills were aimed at preventing "so-called peaceful demonstrations" and went so far as to restrict black voter registration even further than the existing literacy requirements by placing an additional restriction of "good moral character" on applicants. Local registrars would determine who was of good moral character, and more often than not they decided blacks did not qualify.

Registration of black voters, never a high percentage, had dropped precipitously in Mississippi (from an estimated 22,000 to an estimated 8,000) following the Supreme Court decision in 1954 that public schools be integrated. The Mississippi legislature had reacted by passing new laws designed to keep blacks from voting, including requiring voters to pass a test about the state's constitution.

In April, just prior to the Colvards' move to Starkville, ten people were wounded when police and a gang of whites chased blacks from a traditionally all-white beach at Biloxi on the Gulf Coast.

During the week before Colvard was to take over as MSU president, Mississippi Governor Ross Barnett had told the National Governors Conference in a meeting at Glacier National Park in Montana that the federal government had usurped states' rights. "How long will the people of this great nation permit this disgraceful practice and fraud upon the Constitution to continue unrestrained?" Barnett had asked the governors in an obvious reference to so-called federal intervention into Mississippi's affairs.

And during the same week prior to Colvard's arrival, the Jackson *Clarion-Ledger/Daily News* (combined on Sunday) had proclaimed in an editorial: "Real South Resists Compulsory Mixing." In language that would have been difficult to believe in most other parts of the nation, the editorial said, "Despite the hullabaloo and hurrah from integrationists peddling bogus claims that race-mixing is winning increased favor, figures published by *U.S. News & World Report* show that only six percent of colored children are attending integrated schools in the South, although six years have elapsed since mixing was decreed by the Supreme Court."

On the same day the Jackson *Clarion-Ledger* carried an interview with Colvard as the new MSU president, it contained a front page article noting that the State Sovereignty Commission—an official state agency created to guard against federal intrusion—had given its first $20,000 grant of public funds to the Citizens' Councils "to help spread segregation propaganda in its television and radio" forums. In awarding the money to the Citizens' Councils, the Sovereignty Commission Director Albert Jones said, "It merits the active financial support of all patriotic Mississippians who should realize the urgent need for counteracting the one-sided stream of propaganda leveled at the South by most national news media."

In her book *For Us, the Living,* Mrs. Medgar Evers wrote, "What set Mississippi apart was not just the resistance to integration but the fact that the resistance was so great, that people in the state who might dissent were, in any real sense, denied freedom of speech. . . . The tide of progress toward full civil rights, which ebbed and flowed through the rest of the South in those years, caused only minor ripples in Mississippi. Mississippi was a backwater. Mississippi stagnated. The activity, the progress seemed always somewhere else."

Indeed the state was unique in its extremism. "Mississippi is famous for a past of police brutality, and for the sure harassment, even to death, of those who defy the code," historian James W. Silver wrote. "Mississippi's means of governance was more akin to the apartheid system of oppression in South Africa and the fascist system in Hitler's Nazi Germany," political analyst Acie Byrd, Jr., said. Mildred Pitts Walter wrote in *Mississippi Challenge,* "From its early existence, Mississippi was a place where fear, tension, hatred, and hard work were the rule: a place where poor whites struggled against a huge slave labor force that in its discontent created an atmosphere in which the masters felt safe only with an armed militia."

When Colvard took over at MSU, the South was being torn apart, or more accurately its people—black and white—were tearing themselves apart as, for the first time in history, southerners of African American descent were beginning to rise up and demand their civil rights. Although the movement was still in its infancy, it was growing stronger every day, fueled by a chain of events across the South as black leaders used lawsuits to peck away at segregated schools, restaurants, bus stations, hospitals, libraries, employment practices, and housing and voting restrictions.

Violence against blacks was prevalent throughout the state. The Ku Klux Klan was still powerful and active. Mississippi had seen 534 reported lynchings between 1882 and 1952, more than any other state in the nation. In 1960, the median years of school completed by all blacks over the age of twenty-five was just six; 42 percent of whites had finished high school and only 7 percent of blacks.

There were some whites who tried to argue for peaceful obedience to federal law, but their voices were few and far between. Often their businesses were boycotted. Some received anonymous death threats and some were shunned by former friends and church members. A few had their homes or businesses bombed. Mississippi became known as one of the few places in the world where someone could be called a communist for insisting that the (federal) law be upheld.

Colvard was not naive about the problems that might lie ahead. He had been warned that he was entering a potentially volatile situation. The most serious alarm had come from Dr. John Caldwell, his friend and coworker at North Carolina State University in Raleigh, where Colvard had been serving as dean of agriculture and Caldwell was chancellor, appointed in 1959. Caldwell, a native of Mississippi and a graduate of Mississippi State, had been president of the University of Arkansas at Fayetteville in 1957 when President Dwight Eisenhower ordered federal troops into Little Rock, so he knew something of the atmosphere Colvard would be entering. When he found out that Colvard was considering taking the MSU job, Caldwell wrote him a long letter laying out the challenge his friend would be facing. "As one who was raised in Mississippi and who has maintained his connections there with frequent visits," Caldwell wrote, "I can tell you that the president of a state university in Mississippi unavoidably will be confronted, dramatically and intensively, with these great issues of policy, practicality and conscience. It will be unbelievably rough. Little Rock will look like a Sunday School picnic in comparison." He reminded Colvard of University of Alabama Oliver Carmichael's forced resignation following riots at that school in 1956 when a black student named Autherine Lucy was admitted.

It was not that Colvard was ignoring advice from Caldwell and others; he had taken in every word. But there were other factors making him consider taking the job. First of all, Mississippi State needed and wanted him badly because of his background in agricultural science and academic administration. Second, now that the school had received university status, the legislature funneled large amounts of state funds to MSU, realizing that the school was an asset to the state. Despite the ominous signs of racial intolerance all around him, Colvard quietly began the huge tasks confronting him at his new job. "From the beginning, it was apparent that some Mississippians harbored suspicion about the racial stance of the first complete outsider they had ever chosen to be president of Mississippi State University," he wrote in *Mixed Emotions*. "However, the people were among the friendliest we had ever met, and their cordiality almost obscured the occasional hint that we might not conform to the 'true Mississippi way of life.'"

He immediately began to take stock of the quality of his faculty and the physical needs of the campus while at the same time setting up a schedule of speeches to alumni gatherings all across the state. At one of those meetings about a month after Colvard had taken office, an alumnus asked Colvard's traveling companion, alumni secretary Robert Williams, how the new president stood on integration. "Williams told him that he had nothing to worry about, whereupon the alumnus replied that he could go home and sleep well," Colvard wrote. "Exactly what Williams meant by his reply was far from clear to me."

The new president also soon began to call on prominent business leaders in an attempt to build public support for MSU. "What I found in the faculty when I got there were several surprises," Colvard recalled. "They had very much more competent people that I really expected to find." But he also found low salaries and buildings and laboratories in bad need of refurbishing. And he began to discover that Mississippi's reputation on racial matters made it difficult to recruit top professors from other parts of the nation.

Colvard soon learned that he had nearly a free hand with internal budget transfers to alter academic pursuits, but he could not escape the fact that the Board of Trustees of Institutions of Higher Learning in Jackson kept a close eye on everything.

"Number one, I was trying to build what I called a first-class academic program," Colvard recalled. "The other thing I wanted to do was to change the attitudes. They had an inferiority complex. Ole Miss had been the crown jewel of public higher education and Mississippi State had been the cow college. Nobody tried to disclaim, nor did I try to disclaim, a historical agricultural orientation, but I wanted to get rid of that inferiority complex." One of the first things he did was to encourage all teachers to wear coats and ties in class. It was a simple thing, but it helped elevate their position and made them know that he cared about their appearance.

Colvard was succeeding Ben Hilbun, a 1923 MSU graduate who had been registrar for seventeen years before being named president in

1953. He had studied at the University of Toulouse and had an honorary doctoral degree. He had been at MSU since 1925 after having worked two years for the Starkville Chamber of Commerce. Colvard soon discovered that the faculty had been centrally controlled. Thirty-five people reported directly to Hilbun. Former faculty members said he even dealt personally with the man who restocked the soft-drink machines. Despite all the changes he was facing, the new president found he was enjoying life at MSU. "Actually, this may sound strange, but I felt about as relaxed during those first days, first weeks and months as I had in years," he recalled.

His first official speech as MSU's chief executive came on July 12 to an alumni meeting in Greenwood, just seven days after he became president. After Ben Hilbun had introduced him, Colvard said, "Times have changed and almost every change has brought into sharper focus the contributions of and the need for the land-grant university pattern of higher education. More and more people are recognizing that economic expansion does not come about by itself—that it is the result of millions of decisions made by farmers, businessmen, workers, scientists, technicians, and consumers. The work of education and research institutions has contributed to these great advances. If Mississippi is to realize the progress in industrialization, in agricultural and business expansion, of which it is capable, the doors of its land-grant university must be wide open to the young people of this state. Education and research in fields of technology are more expensive than in many other areas. You must see that your university is strong and that its doors are wide open to the young men and women of Mississippi." He went on to tell the Greenwood alumni that MSU and the other sixty-seven land-grant universities enroll more than 20 percent of all college students and train 100 percent of all those who receive doctor's degrees in agriculture and more than 80 percent of those getting bachelor's degrees in agriculture.

Colvard touched on another sensitive subject for the alumni when he said, "A few years from now I hope I may present some impressive statistics on the athletic winning record of your Land-Grant University. As for now, I will say only that I have not had time to learn all of the facts." He pointed out that Mississippi State was very important to the economic future of the entire state. "It cannot fail. To do so would result in retarding the growth of the whole economy and the enrichment of the lives of the people," he said.

"I pledge you my best efforts to mobilize the great talents of your land-grant university faculty to pursue vigorously the educational goals designed to enrich the lives of the people of Mississippi. I shall carry forward with the belief, which I am sure Dr. Hilbun shares, that knowledge for knowledge's sake is not enough but that it must be crowned with commitment to service, to morality and to purpose. We must remember that technological superiority alone will not determine the winner of the conflicts which confront us. They can be won only by a nation of free men—free, encouraged and trained to think for themselves. Trained minds and noble purposes must be companions in our commitment to service. This is the reason the liberal arts were included in the land-grant statement of purpose." He concluded, "We shall do our best to earn your continued support of an able faculty capable of holding their own with the best in the land. I have met with the faculty and find it a responsive body. With your help I shall try to build upon the foundation laid down by my eleven predecessors and to share in their 'firm belief in the nobility of man's search for truth and knowledge' and their 'determination that in that search Mississippi State shall play an important role.'"

After the successful Greenwood appearance, Colvard carefully studied his new situation for a few months and then set about to completely revamp the administration. When he was through he had only six people reporting to him, all vice presidents. He separated academic and administrative duties into two councils. He reorganized all agricultural pursuits under the command of a new vice president of agriculture and forestry and appointed two new deans under him. "He assembled a fairly good team," recalled Dr. Harry Simrall, who was dean of engineering. "He inherited some of us, a good many of us really, but I think there were those of us who were younger or about his age who wanted to move the institution. He had a good feel for what it took and he did a great job in encouraging us. He let you know what he expected you to do and he expected all of us to exert some leadership. We made a good many recommendations for changes, and if he thought it was worth trying, he would let us do it and he helped us to find the money to do it with."

It was not until the beginning of the 1961–62 academic year that Colvard could begin to really put his new team in place. Dr. Herbert Drennon, dean of the university and the graduate school and chair of the English department, retired. Drennon had been on the faculty at MSU since 1919. At this point Colvard was able to institute his new system of vice presidents, and he named Dr. John K. Bettersworth vice president of academic affairs to replace Drennon. Bettersworth, a history professor and author of books on Mississippi history, had been teaching at MSU since 1937. Colvard also brought in Dr. Francis Rhodes from Florida State University to be the new dean of education. In another move designed to seek more federal funds for research, Colvard won consent from the Mississippi Industrial and Technological Research Commission of Jackson, with Governor Barnett's approval, to lend its director, Dr. Andrew Suttle, Jr., to be the part-time coordinator of graduate research at MSU.

Colvard also went to work on a badly needed building program consisting of a women's dormitory, a chemistry building, meats laboratory, aerophysics laboratory, new married-student apartments, and a student union, since MSU had none. Construction of the new engineering research building and the federal entomology laboratory already were under way.

At least one newspaper editor, Oliver Emmerich of the *Jackson State Times*, recognized Colvard's talent as he began his second year at MSU. "It was a day of achievement for Mississippi when Dr. Colvard came to our state," Emmerich wrote on October 1, 1961. "He pinpoints our problems and their solution when he says, 'Research and education set the limits for our progress.'"

Colvard believed in making connections outside the state to enhance MSU's reputation, seek funds, and help him recruit top faculty, so he traveled a lot, leaving his capable assistant, Dr. Ted Martin, in charge. "I never had to worry with Ted Martin taking care of things," Colvard said. Martin was a native Mississippian who had been at Mississippi State since he received his doctorate in school administration from Peabody College in 1949. A broad-shouldered, five-feet eleven-inches tall, the balding Martin was forty-five years old when he started working for Colvard. He wore eyeglasses and smoked a pipe. "He was the ultimate team player," Colvard said.

Martin, a native of Blue Mountain, Mississippi, was the son of a Latin teacher and a Baptist evangelist who went to Dayton, Tennessee, during the famous Scopes "monkey" trial in support of William Jennings Bryan, who had been brought in to prosecute the young teacher for exposing students to the theory of evolution. But Ted Martin was definitely not a supporter of the anti-evolutionist-type thinkers. He worked hard for Colvard and Mississippi State to send the basketball team to Michigan and later to integrate the university. "He thought Dean was very straightforward," Martin's widow, Lorene Martin, recalled years later. "He said Dean was very well organized. They thought alike." Martin died in 1994 at the age of seventy-nine.

Colvard continued to be active in the Association of State Universities and Land-Grant Colleges, particularly its Presidents Council and the American Council on Education. He also was on the board of directors of the Cordell Hull Foundation for International Education, which funded scholarships for students from South America, and the Regional Advisory Council on Graduate Education in Agricultural Science of the Southern Regional Education Board in Atlanta. Colvard justified his travel saying, "We were trying to build programs based on the best in the United States that we could identify. Sometimes we felt that it was better to go to their ground and learn from them directly rather than just depend on the literature."

The best example at MSU was its role in research to develop liquid nitrogen as a fertilizer for various crops. Previously nitrogen had to be added in granular form. The new process was used by MSU alumnus Owen Cooper in his Mississippi Chemical Company at Yazoo City.

While Colvard was traveling, Martha usually stayed home with Wallace, who loved being with Idella Henderson, the cook, and the caretaker, Floyd Minor, who would take him fishing. Martha had many other duties as the president's wife, hosting numerous events for faculty wives and visitors. She also belonged to several clubs, including a federated garden club and the Daughters of the American Revolution, and was a volunteer at the hospital.

In addition to seeking support from alumni and business groups, Colvard significantly stepped up seeking grants from private foundations such as the Rockefeller group in New York. "We started getting successes in the fellowship programs within the National Science Foundation, the National Aeronautics and Space Administration and the (U.S.) Department of Education," recalled Dr. Chester McKee, one of Colvard's appointments as assistant dean of the graduate school (later dean and director of research). "All of that started bringing in money to support graduate students and the programs expanded. It just started rolling."

Colvard's inauguration on April 15, 1961, brought representatives from more than one hundred colleges and universities including Berea, Missouri, North Carolina, and Purdue. Governor Ross Barnett was sitting on the platform to hear speeches by University of Wyoming president Dr. G. D. Humphrey, who was a former MSU president, and Dr. Clifford M. Hardin, chancellor of the University of Nebraska. In his inaugural speech, Colvard said, "As an adopted son of Mississippi, standing on the solid foundation of the state's past achievement and seeking to catch the vision of the future for the institution I am permitted to serve, I can see an ever-widening horizon of opportunity brought into sharp focus by the realities of our time. I have sensed new directions in our agriculture. Muscles of man and beast are giving way to machines; people are moving to towns; higher yields of crops are rewarding the efforts of scientists and educators; vast industries are performing the tasks once dispersed among the farms; the Delta, the Prairies, the Brown Loam, the Clay Hills and the Piney Woods are specializing in crops or in livestock, poultry or forestry with a better understanding of the peculiar advantages of each. The shift from exploitation of our forests to the application of management and scientific culture and the creation of forest industries is easy to see."

Mississippi State had equipped its graduates to acquire not only a better way of life, but also the better things of life, he said. "Mississippi seems ready to enjoy its greatest era in economic expansion," Colvard continued. "The opportunities for the land-grant purpose are far greater than they were one hundred years ago. Our task then will be to mobilize man and his knowledge to a degree that has never been achieved before. We must assemble and make ready for use the best ideas of our time. We must reinforce our moral commitment. We must decide what we can afford to do and what we can afford to leave undone. If we provide in full measure the margin that makes for excellence in a university, we shall require not only the support of the legislature but supplements from other sources." He concluded by saying, "I accept the high responsibility that has been placed upon me today with a deep sense of humility, with a pledge of my full energies to the tasks at hand, and with a plea for the support and cooperation of every one of you. And, at this moment of pledging and pleading, I am moved, not unlike those who raise their hands in solemn oaths, humbly to raise my voice not so much to pledge as to plead—'So help me God!'"

By the end of his first year at MSU, Colvard had started a $15 million building program, the largest by far in the university's history. He also had appointed the university's first dean of women, a new dean of education, new directors of extension, research and graduate studies, a new vice president of agriculture, a new registrar, and a new vice president for academic affairs. His good works did not go unnoticed outside the state. Purdue awarded him an honorary degree in June 1961, and he immediately left for indoctrination for new college and university presidents at Harvard University.

Colvard was not stopping with legislative support. He was surprised to learn that there had never been an organized attempt to raise money for the university outside of its state and federal appropriations. To offset the lack of state funding to raise faculty salaries and pay for key research projects, Colvard came up with an idea—Why not form a private university foundation? He invited sixty prominent alumni and business leaders to a campus meeting on December 9, 1960, to discuss the idea, and they agreed that it should be done.

Tom Jones, a Starkville architect, was one of those invited, but his immediate reaction was negative. "I thought that was the most stupid thing in the world to have a foundation for a public educational institution," Jones recalled. "That's what taxes are for." But he, like others, soon changed his mind after Colvard's speech that night. Jones was impressed when Colvard said, "I'm going to introduce everybody." Jones recalled, "He had hardly met some of those people. Without any notes, he went around the whole room and introduced everyone. That was a brazen thing to pull off, but he did it without any problems." Colvard was pleased with the enthusiasm he found. "This could represent a significant step forward," he noted in his diary. "It is likely to be slow to show concrete results."

After the group of sixty appointed an executive committee of twelve to investigate, Colvard called in Paul H. Davis, a consultant from Los Angeles who had worked with the development program at the University of North Carolina and the Reader's Digest Foundation in New York. Davis visited the MSU campus and told Colvard and the committee that it should not start a foundation until it had enough money to run it for three years. He estimated that would take about $120,000.

After Colvard's inauguration on April 15, 1961, the committee met again and pledged the whole amount. Colvard wondered in his diary: "Will they do it? If they do, this institution will go places. If they do not, it will be difficult to get them steamed up again."

Colvard envisoned the Development Foundation as a means of providing the margin of excellence in terms of supplements for teacher salaries, scholarships, professorships, and buildings.

Greenwood real estate developer Charles Whittington agreed to be the first president of the foundation. But he soon found it was going to be more difficult to raise money than he thought. He enthusiastically sent out letters to 10,000 alumni seeking contributions. "The amount we received would just about have paid the postage of mailing the letters," he recalled. He and Colvard then came up with a plan to designate any person, business, or organization that would pledge $10,000 at once or $1,000 per year for ten years as a Patron of Excellence.

This plan began to work. By late 1962 more than two hundred founding members had contributed the $120,000 in seed money, and the foundation was launched.

The giant was awake.

4 "THANK GOD FOR OLE MISS"

In the fall of 1962, Ole Miss Chancellor John D. Williams was in a bad spot. The courts had ordered the enrollment of James H. Meredith as the first black student in the university's 114-year history, and Governor Ross Barnett had vowed to block it at any cost. A violent confrontation between state and federal officials seemed certain. Barnett had gone on statewide television to declare that Mississippi had the sovereign right to refuse a federal order to desegregate its public facilities. "We must either submit to the unlawful dictates of the federal government or stand up like men and tell them never," the governor had said. "I say we must refuse to submit to illegal usurpation of power by the Kennedy administration. I call upon all public officials, both elected and appointed, to join hands with the people, and resist by every legal and constitutional means the tyrannical edicts which have been and will be directed against the patriotic citizens of our state." Barnett said he was prepared to go to jail for his beliefs and that any state officials who were unwilling to do the same should resign. "Schools will not be closed if this can possibly be avoided, but they will not be integrated," he said.

As the bad news continued to break in daily waves over the Ole Miss situation, MSU President Dean Colvard realized that it very easily could have been his name in the headlines instead of the Ole Miss chancellor's. Despite his many successes at MSU in the past two years, Colvard was a tortured man. He was finding it increasingly more difficult to keep silent while Barnett and other state officials postured—irresponsibly, Colvard felt, in clear defiance of federal law, common sense, and fair play.

Colvard's dilemma was never so sharply defined as when he sat at the same table with Governor Barnett at a luncheon in Jackson on Saturday, September 22, during part of the festivities surrounding the MSU-Florida football game. Barnett was his usual casual, friendly self toward Colvard, although the governor had just personally confronted Meredith to reject his attempt to register at Ole Miss two days before.

Despite their philosophical differences, Colvard and Barnett might have felt a psychic connection. Both had grown up on small farms in the South and both had worked their way through college—Colvard in the dairy at Berea and Barnett as a freelance barber cutting hair in the basement of the science hall at Mississippi College, a private Baptist school in the Jackson suburb of Clinton. Barnett had gone on to law school at Vanderbilt and at Ole Miss before opening his own one-man practice in Jackson. A skilled orator, Barnett considered running for governor in 1947, but decided against it. He entered a six-way race in 1951 and lost. He lost again in 1955, but finally succeeded in 1959, taking office in January 1960. His slogan was "Roll with Ross, He's His Own Boss," implying that his opponent was taking orders from a former governor.

Barnett, like all the other candidates for governor, emphasized his anti-integration stance. "We can solve our own problems," Barnett told his campaign crowds. "Thinking people of both races can work on solutions that will enable us to grow in progress. But we will not, and cannot, ever let our country become as mongrelized as Egypt, where a cultural nation allowed itself to integrate with inferior races that brought about its downfall." But Barnett also promised to bring new industry into the state, and he was backed by the powerful Mississippi Manufacturers Association for his pledge for a right-to-work law and more exclusionary workers' compensation laws.

Several people came up to Barnett at the luncheon at the Capital City Club in Jackson to congratulate him on his bold public statements that Mississippi would defy any attempt to enroll Meredith. The fact that Barnett apparently assumed Colvard to be of like mind on the racial situation tortured Colvard all the while.

"I am torn between a sense of responsibility to keep quiet and try to maintain a reasonable stability at M.S.U. and a feeling that I should resign," Colvard wrote in his diary. "It is clearly evident that I cannot continue to live and work with success and happiness in this environment. It will be next to impossible to recruit top staff and do an educational job. On the other hand I do not wish to run away while there is instability. Being an 'outsider' few people are discussing the issues with me. This is fortunate. I believe the U.S. Courts have acted on the racial issue without full recognition of the depth of unreadiness for full integration. On the other hand, since the courts have ruled, the people are being encouraged to rebel against even a moderate compliance. Thus the conflict. I am praying for strength to so conduct myself as to remain calm, to be honest with my own convictions and to help in any way I can to cause the good in our people to emerge—I wish I knew how to turn the strong tide of hate into a tide of love—or how to switch off emotionalism and mob tendencies and to switch on rationality and good judgment." In his methodical, meticulous manner, Colvard drew up plans in his head for the day when integration would become his problem at MSU.

As Colvard waited at Starkville, the situation worsened at Oxford. Federal officials were to bring Meredith to the Ole Miss campus on Sunday, September 30, and a call went out over the media asking for a show of force by Mississippians. The university's chief executive, J. D. Williams, who had been chancellor at Ole Miss since 1946, had called for calm and order on the campus, but his role had been superseded by the governor.

"Our students were beginning to show restlessness," Colvard wrote in his diary. "They were responding to some of the television programs asking for a 'pilgrimage' of people to Oxford to support Gov. Barnett. Some students phoned to see if we would declare a holiday Monday for them to go. . . . I told them there would be no holiday and urged them to keep cool and stay on the campus." About one hundred MSU students gathered around the statue of founder Lee on Sunday night chanting and shouting anti-integration slogans. They marched into downtown Starkville still chanting, but after that the crowd broke up and there were no further incidents.

All hell broke loose on the Ole Miss campus that Sunday night. Two people were killed in the riots that followed Meredith's admission as a student. Federal officials called in 22,000 National Guard and regular Army troops. Fifteen of Colvard's MSU students were arrested on the Ole Miss campus. One of them was Lawrence Mellin, who had gone to the Ole Miss campus out of curiosity with his friend, another Mississippi State student, Bud Sanderson. "We had heard President Kennedy on TV and we marched downtown. Then Bud and I decided to go to Oxford," Mellin recalled years later.

When they got to Oxford, Mellin and Sanderson joined a crowd of hundreds of other students rallying around retired General Edwin Walker, who had called for all true Southerners to show up at Oxford as a protest to federal intervention. Mellin said one of the National Guardsmen was hit by a thrown brick and dropped his rifle, so Mellin picked it up and put it in the trunk of his car. He then walked back to campus and told a Guardsman that he had found the rifle. Troops accompanied him back to the car, retrieved the rifle and detained Mellin and Sanderson for questioning. They were held overnight without being charged with any crime. The next day Mellin was in class at Mississippi State when Colvard had him called to his office. "I just wanted to know what had gone on up there," Colvard recalled. Mellin said he was glad to cooperate with Colvard because he respected him. "He stood up for us," Mellin said. "We students were fond of both him and Mrs. Colvard."

President Kennedy had gone on television for a national speech just as the first tear gas canisters were being fired. "Had the police powers of Mississippi been used to support the orders of the court, instead of deliberately and unlawfully blocking them," Kennedy said, "had the University of Mississippi fulfilled its standard of excellence by quietly admitting this applicant in conformity with what so many other southern state universities have done for so many years, a peaceable and sensible solution would have been possible without any federal intervention."

Governor Barnett ordered the Mississippi state flag at half staff, saying "there had been an invasion of our state resulting in blood." Colvard wrote in his diary, "It will take years for Ole Miss and Mississippi to recover. While this chaos has prevailed I have had to exercise great restraint to keep from speaking out in some ways not calculated to be popular in Mississippi."

Later he wrote in *Mixed Emotions*, "While I had succeeded in keeping Mississippi State University on a relatively steady course, it was sobering to realize that this confrontation could have happened on our campus and that our turn at bat would come all too soon. The national news had been so traumatic that friends in some other universities were offering to bail me out if the situation became so unbearable that I decided to resign or to have my contract with MSU otherwise terminated. I had letters or telegraphs from both NC State and the University of Florida that they were holding a job open for me if it got so bad I couldn't stand it in Mississippi."

Mississippi's reputation indeed had taken another blow as Colvard soon discovered. He flew to Chicago three days after the Oxford riots to attend the annual meeting of the American Council on Education. "In the Congress Hotel where the meetings were held I was tempted to remove my name tag," he wrote. "When the delegates saw that I was from Mississippi they wanted to talk—or in some instances they looked upon me with some expression of aloofness, sympathy or superiority. Even four farmers from New Zealand who saw the name of the state when we went up on the elevator invited me in their room. They were not part of the convention." To add insult to injury, the council passed a resolution condemning the political involvement of Governor Barnett in the operation of the university. (Despite Barnett's popularity at the time of the Ole Miss incident in 1962, he was defeated when he tried to be elected governor again in 1967.)

Colvard returned to Starkville with a heavy heart, but still unsure of what to do. He felt the Ole Miss publicity would hurt his chances of recruiting top academic talent, and he was proved correct. Within a few days of the riots, MSU received a turndown letter from an assistant professor at the University of Chicago. "I do not hesitate to say that one factor in this is the attitude and behavior of students, faculty, and the citizens of Mississippi," Robert Connor wrote. "I realize that Oxford and State College are separate, but I don't feel my wife and I would be happy in such an atmosphere."

Colvard wrote in his diary that he was discouraged, but determined to continue. "It is a shame for a state so much in need of top quality higher education to have its already lagging programs even further retarded. Everybody is trying to blame somebody else."

Within a few weeks, another crisis loomed when the Southern Association of Colleges and Schools sent a warning to Governor Barnett that all public four-year colleges and universities in Mississippi would be removed from the accredited list unless the association could be assured that political interference would not occur again. Such a loss of accreditation would mean that all the colleges and universities in Mississippi, including MSU, would have their academic programs removed from the association's rolls.

Colvard had been anticipating such a threat. On October 27, he spoke to a group of High School Day visitors on the MSU campus saying everyone should be concerned with the possible loss of accreditation, but he was positive that steps would be taken to make sure that did not happen. He also said, "I wish to commend our students for the restraint they have displayed under some of the tense conditions which have prevailed in our state." He repeated his assurances about accreditation in a speech on November 2 to the Starkville Rotary Club and received a resounding ovation when he added, "At this point let me make it clear that the agitators for forced integration will receive no comfort from me. Let me also make it equally clear that I shall do everything in my power to prevent any violence from occurring on this campus resulting from this problem or from any other."

He was surprised to receive a compliment the next day from Governor Barnett who was visiting on campus. "It had not been calculated to please either him or the Citizens Council," Colvard wrote in *Mixed Emotions*. "The general reaction on campus and in the community to what I had said seemed very good. I had to confess some uncertainty as to whether the people were changing their attitudes or whether they failed to understand the message intended in my comments. At least it was encouraging to feel that I had enough support to keep a semblance of solidarity within the university and perhaps in the community."

Colvard flew to Dallas on November 24 along with other MSU officials and governing board members to argue that accreditation not be lifted. The association decided to put all four-year institutions in Mississippi on "extraordinary" status with the condition that any further political interference would result in loss of approved status.

"With some reluctance I agreed with this recommendation," Colvard wrote. "In a way it seemed unfair to punish other institutions for actions taken at Ole Miss, actions over which others had no control. On the other hand, the violations had been committed largely by the governor. He had interfered with the authority of the board of trustees which had administrative responsibility for all public senior colleges and universities. Any effort to secure a more favorable treatment for Mississippi State would not have been successful, and if successful, it might have resulted in Ole Miss getting more severe treatment." Colvard said later he could not conclude with certainty how he would have handled this type of confrontation with political demagoguery if the situation had arisen first at the MSU campus instead of at Ole Miss.

Colvard's mood was bordering on morose when he returned to MSU only to face more problems as the year wound down. "My annual athletic problem came into focus," Colvard told his diary. "Wade Walker's contract expires July 1, 1963. There is considerable agitation among some of the alumni to fire him as athletic director." MSU students and alumni had been howling mad about the university's dismal record in football, and the time had come for Colvard to do something about it. Although Walker had been an All-American at the University of Oklahoma as a player, his teams had not won a single SEC game in three years. Colvard had stood behind him as head coach at the end of the 1960 season, despite a 2-6-1 record. He conferred with Walker and announced his support until he had been president long enough to have a more complete understanding of the athletic program. The dissidents reluctantly accepted that decision. When 1961 ended with five wins and five losses, he took away his head coaching duties and left him only as athletic director. After the 1962 season ended with three wins and six losses, he kept him as athletic director at a reduced salary and gave him a year-to-year contract.

His problems with the football program were still very much on Colvard's mind as he entered 1963, but an unexpected achievement in academics gave him a boost. Selected from seventy nominations, MSU's team of four students won its first round in the General Electric College Bowl competition televised by CBS in New York City on Sunday, January 13, 1963. The team defeated the Pratt Institute team from Brooklyn and returned to New York the following week to compete against a team from the Drexel Institute of Philadelphia. MSU lost that round, but the team had gathered positive national publicity for once for MSU and the state of Mississippi. Yazoo City industrialist Owen Cooper, an MSU alumnus and ardent Colvard supporter, was so pleased that he hosted a "Varsity Scholars" dinner for the four team members, two alternates, and faculty coach.

Cooper was president of Mississippi Chemical Corporation, a firm that sold liquid nitrogen to farmers. A 1929 graduate of MSU, he had been named alumnus of the year in 1960. He held a law degree from the Jackson School of Law and had also done graduate work at the University of Southern California. A deacon of his Baptist church in Yazoo City, he also was president of the board of trustees of the New Orleans Theological Seminary. His dinner for the College Bowl team attracted wide publicity across Mississippi. "In addition to honoring them," Colvard noted in his diary, "a major purpose was to place academic performance in a more prominent position in the public image of MSU and to emphasize to student leaders the importance of maintaining a proper academic environment." The banquet, attended by more than one hundred student leaders, several faculty members, alumni, and business leaders, was a tonic for Colvard. "If and when a Negro is admitted to MSU," he wrote, "this meeting might well represent a turning point in attitudes. It is far from certain at this writing what the future will bring."

It was at this point that Colvard had to make his decision about whether the MSU basketball team should be allowed to break the "unwritten rule." As champions of the SEC they had earned an invitation to the regional National Collegiate Athletic Association tournament to compete for the national title. The so-called unwritten law had been adopted after fallout from the *Brown v. Board of Education* decision. MSU had played a game in 1956 against an integrated team during an invitational tournament at Evansville, Indiana, but the team was ordered to come home before the second game, also against an integrated team, could be played. "We did not know beforehand there would be Negroes in the tournament," said then–MSU athletic director C. R. "Dudy" Noble, who ordered the withdrawal.

A year later, the University of Mississippi team walked out of the All-American City Basketball tournament in Owensboro, Kentucky, rather than play an Iona College team that had one black player. "When we accepted the invitation to that tournament, it was with an understanding that there would be no Negroes in it," Ole Miss athletic director C. M. "Tad" Smith said. Host Wesleyan College president Dr. Oscar W. Leber pointed out that Ole Miss had played in the tournament in 1954 against teams with black players. The game went down in the record books as a 2-0 victory for Iona.

Colvard had several reasons for wanting the team to compete. First of all, it would give a positive boost to the MSU and Mississippi image. Second, he felt that the four seniors on the team deserved a chance after having played together for three years and having won the SEC championship all three times. To many outsiders, the coach and the team would not appear to favor integration-oriented sports. McCarthy, who was in his seventh year as head coach at MSU, was a thirty-nine-year-old native of Baldwyn, a hamlet just north of Tupelo in the northeast corner of the state. All but two of the twelve players on the 1962–63 squad were sons of the South. Nine were from Mississippi, one from Kentucky, and two from Illinois.

It was a powerful team that had mastered the art of the slowdown as well as deadeye shooting. Coach McCarthy had predicted in 1960 that the members of his undefeated freshman team with a 21-0 record would win the SEC championship when they joined the varsity. Four of the five freshmen players became starters the next year and brought home the SEC crown. They did the same the following year and again in their senior year. "This crew has been almost a coach's dream," McCarthy said.

All twelve team members were on record as wanting to compete in Michigan. "I don't see anything morally wrong playing against Negroes, Indians, Russians or any other race or nationality," Leland Mitchell, a 6'-4" forward and the leading rebounder and coleader in scoring, told the media. "Most of the boys have played against them in high school or in hometown sandlot games. In my opinion it's just like playing against anyone else. You consider him just another player." Mitchell came from Kiln, Mississippi, near the Gulf Coast, just a few miles from Poplarville, where a black man, Mack Charles Parker, had been lynched in 1959 when Mitchell was a senior in high school.

Bobby Shows, a 6'-7" center from Brookhaven, Mississippi, said he did not think that just playing a team with Negroes constituted integration. "In my opinion, playing against them up there won't be a form of integration because we'll be playing against them and playing to beat them," he said. "I think the majority of the people want us to go. In a democracy, the majority is supposed to rule." Joe Dan Gold, a 6'-5" forward from Benton, Kentucky, said he thought the team ought to go to Michigan because "it would make the whole state of Mississippi look less prejudiced and it would make it appear the state is trying to work out a solution to its problem of competing on the same level for national championships and prestige." W. D. "Red" Stroud, a 6'-1" set-shot whiz from Forest, said it would give MSU a chance to win the national championship.

Doug Hutton, a junior 5'-10" guard from Jackson, said that to deny the invitation would take away incentive to win future championships. Don Posey, a sophomore forward from Indianola, said, "Since we have gained the privilege to go, we should be allowed to. Our going would then bring prestige to the school and to the team. It is a great honor to compete with other top teams in the nation and I hope we are able to attain that honor." Junior forward Stan Brinker and sophomore forward Richie Williams, both from Metropolis, Illinois, said they wanted to go. "I've played against Negroes before," Brinker said. "After you get out on the court, they're just ball players and part of another team you are trying to beat." Williams said, "I've competed against integrated teams as well as having played on them in high school and it hasn't affected my play or my feeling against integration."

Despite their comments, the MSU players had not practiced while all the jockeying for approval had been going on, convinced that the unwritten law would prevail. "We still didn't think we were going, even in our senior year," Mitchell recalled. "Coach McCarthy certainly didn't think we were going because we weren't even practicing."

When the word finally came down that they were going, the Maroon Bulldogs realized that was only a beginning. Their first opponent was to be Loyola of Chicago, ranked fourth in the nation with a 24-2 record and averaging more than 100 points a game. As winner of the SEC championship, MSU, ranked seventh nationally with a 25-1 record, had a first-round bye in the regional tournament, but the Loyola Ramblers had whipped Tennessee Tech 111-42 in the first-round game at Evanston, Illinois. The winner of the regional tournament would go on to Lexington, Kentucky, for the Final Four competition.

Meanwhile, on Thursday afternoon, the day before the big game, NCAA officials waited anxiously at the East Lansing airport for the MSU flight to arrive. It was late and rumors had begun to fly that the Mississippi team had been pulled back at the last minute, but fog had only delayed the takeoff. Finally, the plane landed at 3:00 P.M., and a relieved NCAA official greeted McCarthy: "Coach, there's quite a gathering here. A lot of folks are looking for you." McCarthy quipped, "There are a lot of people looking for me where I came from, too." One headline read, "NCAA Officials Finally at Ease after Mississippi State Lands."

Although it was a moot point, the injunction that Senator Billy Mitts had sought was finally ordered invalid by the Mississippi Supreme Court on that same day, March 14.

Because of all the publicity, the Maroon Bulldogs were the Cinderellas of the tournament. Newsmen and photographers from all over the nation hounded them, pleading for poses and colorful quotes from the brave boys from down in the Deep South. Nashville *Tennessean* sports writer John Bibb wrote: "Around here [East Lansing], most people have adopted the Bulldogs as underdog favorites, and they very likely will have the support of much of the crowd tonight. State is considered a pioneering outfit, battling extreme odds." Even Loyola's coach, George Ireland, was quoted as saying, "I feel Mississippi State has a right to be here, no matter what the segregationists say. They may be the best basketball team in the nation and if they are, they have a right to prove it."

Years later, Ireland told the *Chicago Tribune* that he had withheld mentioning threats from Ku Klux Klan types against his own team with its four black starters. He said he was proud of both teams, but saluted Mississippi State for its courageous effort. "That was the Deep South coming in and saying it was time to end this."

One of Ireland's black players, Jerry Harkness, chosen an All-American that year, recalled threats before the game with MSU. "When we went up against Mississippi State, there was still pressure from the Klan," he said in the *Chicago Tribune* story. "They were sending us letters that we better not even play. Meanwhile, the black community was saying we better not lose."

Both teams were nervous when they took to the floor before the crowd of 12,000 in Michigan State's Jenison Field House. Joe Dan Gold recalled, "I was the team captain and I went out to shake hands with Harkness and about a thousand flashbulbs went off." MSU jumped out to an early 7-0 lead, but Loyola soon caught up and put the Maroons down 26-19 at halftime. State pulled to within 30-27 as the second half got under way, but soon fell behind for good. Mitchell, who finished with 14 points, fouled out with six minutes left. The final score was 61-51, far below Loyola's 100-point average. "It was a rough, tough game," Mitchell said. "This was a physical game, but it was a clean game." Coach McCarthy told the press, "The guys played their hearts out and lost to a better ball club." When someone asked if the black-white confrontation was a factor in MSU's loss, he replied, "The color didn't make any difference. I don't even want to talk about that because it wasn't important."

The next night MSU took to the floor in the tournament's consolation game against Bowling Green of Ohio, champions of the Mid-America Conference and one of the two teams that previously had beaten Loyola that season. This time the MSU Bulldogs were victorious, 65-60, and ended the season ranked sixth in the nation. Loyola won the tournament 79-64 over Big Ten cochampion Illinois. The Ramblers then went on to defeat Duke in the semifinals at Lexington and win the national championship 60-58 in overtime against defending champion Cincinnati University. Mitchell, who scored 23 points in the Bowling Green win, was the only Maroon voted to the All-Tournament Team at East Lansing. Also named to the team was Bowling Green's star, 6'-11" Nate Thurmond, who had 31 rebounds in the loss to MSU.

The national press had a field day with the matchups. *Chicago American* sports columnist Bill Gleason wrote, "Mississippi State managed to make everybody happy—integrationists, segregationists and basketball fans. State's players did all these things by losing to Loyola's four Negro starters, by defeating Bowling Green's three Negro starters and by winning the third place trophy." Gleason was the newspaperman who said he thought the tournament at East Lansing was the most important thing that had happened in American sports since Jackie Robinson broke into major-league baseball. Robinson became the first black player in professional baseball when he starred for the Brooklyn Dodgers in 1947.

The Maroon Bulldogs were met by an enthusiastic crowd of more than 1,000 when they returned to Starkville. After welcoming remarks by Bob Taylor, president of the MSU student body, and Dr. D. W. Aiken, dean of student affairs, Coach McCarthy made a few remarks and read some congratulatory telegrams, including one from Kentucky Coach Adolph Rupp. Then the players signed some autographs and it was over.

Years later Mitchell would recall that, despite the number of avowed segregationists in the state at the time, no one had ever said a negative word to him about going. Colvard's decision to send the team to the tournament had a dramatic effect on the future of higher education in Mississippi, former governor William Winter recalled. "It was the first real breakthrough after the Brown decision of 1954," he said. "It was a recognition at the highest levels in academia that our schools could no longer endure a totally segregated environment. . . . Dr. Colvard had the courage and understanding of so many people in the state that the time had finally come to defy that unwritten rule."

Colvard's former public information director, Bob Moulder, said, "It paved the way for Mississippi State to participate in athletics with other teams throughout the country." Moulder was thirty-five years old when Colvard decided to send the 1963 team to Michigan. He had come to MSU in 1957 from his job as a reporter for the *Clarion-Ledger* in Jackson. Moulder could have been expected to have been a segregationist, having had Erle Johnston as his Scoutmaster in Boy Scouts when he was a youth in Forest. His father had gone to college with Ross Barnett. "Yes, I was nervous," he recalled later. "We were determined that it wasn't going to happen to us. When Dr. Colvard made that decision I was very proud of him. All of us wanted the team to go. Ole Miss was first and we saw what happened. Had Mississippi State been the first, it might have happened there."

Colvard said he had decided not to go to East Lansing to watch his boys play the game of their lives because he was scheduled to give the Auburn University commencement address that Saturday, and besides, "the coach and athletic director are quite capable of handling those things." He listened to the Loyola game on the radio at Auburn that night and noted, "Our boys were a little stiff." Immediately after his speech, he and his family left to visit relatives in North Carolina, and he, Martha, and Wallace returned to MSU on that Sunday night after the basketball team had arrived earlier that day.

Most of the Mississippi press either endorsed or at least grudgingly accepted the groundbreaking event, but some editors still called it a big mistake. Just twenty miles north of Starkville, *West Point News* columnist Henry Shavers wrote: "Since the Mississippi State basketball team went to the integrated national tournament, we're glad they made a good showing. But, for one, we hope that's the last of it. Mississippi's cause for segregation has been drastically hurt during the past few days." The *Copiah County News* in Hazlehurst called for the legislature to outlaw any future such games. "It is amazing that people who become over-enthusiastic about sports will allow themselves to lose all sense of reason as was done in the matter of the MSU basketball team playing in the NCAA tournament," the paper said in editorial. "By the use of trickery, and evading summons, the coach managed to get the team out of the state and to the tournament. They played a team consisting of four Negro and one white players. They lost, which was no surprise to anyone. And, they returned to Mississippi and brought with them nothing but disgrace to our fair state. If they had won, they would have still disgraced the State of Mississippi. The team destroyed a precedent that has been honored by Mississippians since the public school system began. What those young men, their coaches, Dr. Colvard and others guilty of this disgraceful incident, do on their own is their business, but they represented, in this case, the State of Mississippi and they did something that not many full blooded Mississippians would have done."

The MSU student newspaper, the *Reflector*, was appreciative in its editorial. "The president of our university received a genuine proving ground at the beginning of this year, and he showed us all that he is behind the students all the way. . . . We do not know whether the president has much personal interest in the game of basketball, but we do know that he will stand up for us in a manner he deems fit. Only a possum player would believe that the road ahead in Mississippi will be an easy one. It makes us, who hold this university dear to our hearts, feel confident to think that we have a staunch helmsman to lead us over troubled waters which may be ahead of us."

The editorial writer did not know how prophetic his words would be. From that date no serious objections were raised when athletic teams in the SEC were matched against integrated or all-black teams. But that was only the beginning of the impact of the end of the unwritten law, although it would be twenty-eight years before the MSU Bulldogs would return to the NCAA regional tournament.

5
PREPARING FOR
INTEGRATION

After his basketball team had lost the Loyola game and won national prestige and respect, President Colvard was pleased but eager to get on with building the university. "When I made the decision to send them to the playoffs, I fully expected that my usefulness in Mississippi could be destroyed," Colvard recalled. "As it turned out I survived the barrage of hateful epithets and came out of the situation stronger than when I made the decision. We lost the game but gained a great deal of national acclaim. This represented a major breakthrough in racial policy in Mississippi."

Still some of Colvard's opponents were not satisfied. On Thursday following the tournament weekend in Michigan, his old nemesis M. M. Roberts made another attempt to squelch him when the Board of Trustees of Institutions of Higher Learning held its regular meeting in Jackson. Roberts introduced a motion, backed by three other diehard segregationists, to have all "controversial" matters referred to the full board, another obvious attempt to block any future preemptive moves. The motion failed by a vote of seven to four.

Colvard noted in his diary: "I believe we have now about finished with this episode—with some scars but with a feeling that the right thing was done and that in the long run this action will be good for Mississippi. Many good people have rallied to our support and only time will tell the rest of the story." He quickly resumed his normal schedule, which included meeting with alumni groups and the boards and committees of national organizations he served on. In early April, he attended the joint committee of National Association of State Universities and Land-Grant Colleges and the U.S. Department of Agriculture in Washington. And while he was there he testified before the House and Senate hearings on the importance of agriculture experiment stations and extension services.

While continuing his heavy meeting schedule and battling with legislative committees to get more money for MSU, Colvard again turned to work on the Mississippi Development Foundation.

Mr. and Mrs. F. C. White of Okolona came forward in early 1962 with the first substantial gift, 1,000 acres of farm and forest land worth $250,000. The Patrons of Excellence idea also was gaining strength.

Meanwhile, as public universities in Alabama, Georgia, and South Carolina continued to receive their first black students, Colvard was more convinced than ever that MSU's turn would be only a matter of time, and he started to make plans for that eventuality.

Violence continued to plague Mississippi. In April 1963 a white protester was killed trying to march from Chattanooga to Jackson to give a letter to Governor Ross Barnett asking him to work for racial harmony. On May 28, 1963, four students and a white professor from Tougaloo College staged a sit-in at Woolworth's lunch counter in Jackson. It had been orchestrated by Medgar Evers, the NAACP chief representative in Mississippi. Within a few days, six hundred black protesters were in Jackson jails. Mississippi again made national and international news when Evers was gunned down and murdered on June 11, 1963, on his front porch in Jackson. Demonstrations erupted the next day in the downtown area. "If there ever had been a question as to the outcome, it should have been clear by this time that qualified blacks would be admitted to any state university to which they applied," Colvard wrote in *Mixed Emotions*.

During that summer of 1963, Birmingham, Alabama, added to the South's image problems as police used dogs and fire hoses to suppress protesting blacks. Also during that summer, future Democratic candidate for vice president Joseph Lieberman visited Mississippi to help blacks register to vote as a student from Yale University. "For the first time in my life, I was uneasy, even fearful, in the white community and comfortable and secure in the black community," he recalled in an interview with the *New York Times* thirty-seven years later.

Colvard became convinced that even more violence would erupt if federal officials did not slow down and take a more deliberate approach to integration of public facilities. For this reason, he turned down an invitation from President Kennedy in June 1963 to come to the White House to discuss proposed civil rights legislation. Several other southern college and university leaders did attend. "The Kennedys seem to have encouraged demonstrations which have led to riots," Colvard wrote in his diary.

Despite the racial unrest and his continuing fights with the governing board in Jackson, Colvard felt that 1963 had been a good year for him and for MSU. The football team had finally posted a winning season at 7-2-1 and even played in the Liberty Bowl at Philadelphia. The opponent was Colvard's old school, NC State. "Barnett could not be persuaded to stay home, and the NAACP threatened to picket the game," John Bettersworth wrote in his history of Mississippi State. "Actually, the only fracas was on the gridiron, where Mississippi State whipped N.C. State 16-12."

Colvard's influence was being felt on campus in more areas than just academics. The student newspaper, the *Reflector*, said in a May 1964 editorial, "No one has Mississippi State more at heart than President Colvard. He has shown us this on many occasions, one of which made him the center of a controversy resulting from his decision to let the basketball team compete in the NCAA." The editorial, written by student editor Malcolm Balfour, called for support of Colvard's comments urging no violence if and when the university was confronted with integration. "There is a definite possibility that a Negro will apply to enter this university in the near future and none of us should be caught by surprise," the editorial continued. "If all legitimate, honorable, and legal resistance does fail and we get our backs to the wall and face a court order backed by the power of the United States government, then we have the ultimate alternatives of operating Mississippi State as a first-class desegregated institution or of operating Mississippi State as a second-class desegregated institution. These are the only ultimate alternatives."

In 1964, Colvard found that his work in several national organizations and the notoriety MSU had received as a result of the NCAA appearance at Michigan meant he was on the road more than ever as a guest speaker or visiting expert, and he soon found himself being courted for other high-level jobs. His calendar began to fill up with appointments in Georgia, North Carolina, Texas, New Mexico, Colorado, Wyoming, Kansas, West Virginia, Arkansas, Tennessee, Alabama, California, and Washington, D.C. Within the span of a just a few months in 1964, feelers of job offers came to him to fill the chief executive's office at the University of Idaho, the University of Wyoming, the University of Missouri at Kansas City, Florida State University, Oklahoma State University, Auburn University, and his alma mater of Berea College. In July Colvard was on vacation with his family on the North Carolina coast when his old friend, Bill Friday, president of the consolidated University of North Carolina system, called to ask if he would be interested in becoming chancellor of a new university branch being created in Charlotte. Colvard told him he was.

As the year wore on, others sought Colvard as a candidate. The University of Georgia interviewed him for the vice chancellor for research and development position, and he was contacted about becoming dean of tropical agriculture at the University of Hawaii. The Ford Foundation wanted to know if he would help develop agriculture programs in Colombia and Venezuela, and the Rockefeller Foundation asked him to consider working for one of its programs in Thailand or Nigeria. In August he was part of a group of southern educational leaders who had lunch at the White House with President Lyndon Johnson, who had called them together to help support his War on Poverty.

It was a heady time for the boy from Grassy Creek.

Eventually the word leaked out that Colvard had let it be known that he might be in the market for a new job, and MSU backers began dangling incentives in front of him to try to keep him in Starkville. Supporters offered him a $100,000 annuity and a new Cadillac. They renewed his four-year contract for his state salary. Some even asked him to consider running for governor and pledged their support to raise money for such a campaign. He dismissed this as a gesture of support, not as a realistic alternative.

Perhaps the most unusual offer was the one from Auburn. Governor George Wallace, who had "stood in the schoolhouse door" in a symbolic gesture to prevent integration at the University of Alabama, even sent his plane to pick up Colvard and fly him to the state capital of Montgomery, where he pressed Colvard to take the Auburn presidency. The chairman of the Auburn board of trustees flew to Starkville to talk to Colvard about the presidency. Colvard told him he wasn't interested and recommended an Auburn graduate he had hired at NC State by the name of E. T. York. The Auburn board wouldn't give up that easily, though, and asked Colvard for another interview and he complied, but he still wasn't interested. Then the editor of *Southern*

Living magazine, O. B. Copeland, who was another of Colvard's former associates at NC State, called to say that Governor Wallace was going to call Colvard, which he did. "I told him that I hadn't changed my position, but I certainly won't refuse to talk to the governor of a southern state about a very fine institution that I believed to be important," Colvard recalled. So Wallace sent an Alabama state plane to pick him up and fly him to the Alabama capital of Montgomery for an interview in the governor's office.

The Alabama legislature was in session at the time, so as Wallace and Colvard talked, various legislators popped in and out of the governor's office seeking his approval on important matters of state. "He told me the board had agreed on me unanimously and offered me $2,000 more than the committee of the Auburn board had," Colvard recalled. "I said, 'Well, Governor, I've heard you had some pretty sharp things to say about the federal government. Auburn was created as a partnership between the federal and state government. You've been talking about not accepting federal funds and if I was going to be the president of Auburn University I would be very much interested in what the position of the governor was since the governor also is chairman of the board of trustees.' At that point, Wallace jerked forward in his chair and quickly replied, 'Doctor, I'll tell you just exactly where I stand on that. I want you to accept every damned cent you can get, but I don't want anybody to act like they enjoy it.'"

The meeting ended with Colvard telling Wallace he would go back to Starkville and think about the governor's offer, but in reality he already had made up his mind not to accept, and he waited a few days before calling Wallace to tell him so. "He knew about my racial stance regarding the basketball team's playing in Michigan, but the tide was turning and he was a good politician," Colvard said.

Although he was no longer governor, Barnett had fanned the flames again in May of 1964, on the tenth anniversary of the *Brown v. Board of Education* decision. The editors of *Newsday* in New York had asked him to write a first-person essay on why he opposed integration. "When the real results of these ten years of expensive effort are analyzed, it appears, quite frankly, that the integrationists have been accepting money and support under false pretenses," Barnett wrote. "For despite ten years of intensive agitation, school integration has made hardly a dent in the Deep South." He argued that only 1.06 percent of the blacks in the eleven states of the Old Confederacy were attending schools that previously had been all white. "This means that school integration is proceeding at the rate of a scant one-tenth of one percent per year—which would require 1,000 years to achieve 100 percent mixing of the races in the schools," Barnett wrote. All the easy court-ordered victories had already been achieved, and integration in the future would be even tougher to achieve, he said. "And I am proud to point out that my own state of Mississippi remains untouched; her people are united in their determination to retain control of their own local affairs—including the pubic schools."

The negative atmosphere had heated up again in June when three civil rights workers were declared missing at Philadelphia, Mississippi, just sixty miles south of Starkville. The case was so controversial that President Lyndon Johnson sent former Central Intelligence Agency director Allen Dulles to Mississippi to urge Governor Paul Johnson's full cooperation in seeking the three young men, two white and one black. The FBI was called in and gave the case the code name "Mississippi Burning." A Hollywood movie with that title was made years later about the incident.

"The eyes of the world are focused again upon this state and the picture they see is not a pretty one," Colvard wrote in his diary after he had read about the three missing men. A week later they were still missing, and Colvard wrote, "My opinion is that they are dead. There are about 400 of these students in the state. It may be predicted that there will be further violence before the summer ends."

Forty-four days after the young men had disappeared, their bodies were found under a dam near Philadelphia. Again, Mississippi was on the national nightly television news. The FBI reported that thirty-seven black churches had been burned in 1964, sixteen in Pike County alone, apparently in retaliation for having been used for civil rights meetings.

Colvard personally had opposed the Mississippi Summer Project campaign that led to the three deaths. He was convinced that federal legislation and court orders were getting the job done and that activity proposed by the Mississippi Summer Project would be counterproductive, inflammatory, and lead to more violence. He felt so strongly that he argued against allowing the training of the civil rights workers to go on at his old alma mater, Berea College. (Eventually the Berea board voted not to allow the training.) "While I felt confident that Mississippians considered me a liberal on the race question, I had the feeling that my friends at Berea College regarded me as a conservative on this matter," Colvard wrote. "I was sure that few would leave room for a moderate position; however, I thought we had reached the point where civil disobedience should be discouraged."

To his later regret, Colvard never had the opportunity to discuss any of the developments during the sixties with any black leader in Mississippi because he had no relationship with one. "There simply weren't any that I knew," he said later. "Unfortunately, most of the contacts between black leaders and the white establishment were either adversarial or collaborative. There was very little opportunity for low-key, rational discussion and give and take. My hope was that my public support for justice and rationality would achieve better results than heated talk."

The passing of the federal Civil Rights Act in July 1964 meant Colvard and the chief executives of the other public colleges and universities would have to sign assurances of compliance before federal funds would be forthcoming. Colvard was concerned because MSU's $18 million annual budget contained $7 million in federal money. "Failure to sign the assurances of compliance could bring about financial disaster," Colvard wrote. He was frustrated when the governing board reacted negatively and tried to find a way to wriggle out of complying. "While federal control was the talking point, it seemed clear that integration was the real issue." But even then, Colvard and others knew that failure to sign would not prevent integration, since separate court action could bring that about. "Many of us concluded that the real question was whether we should have integration with federal funds or integration without federal funds."

The governing board eventually took an unexpected route. It voted 10-1 to inform the federal government that it was under a court order to comply with the Civil Rights Act and authorized Colvard and the other college and university presidents to sign any emergency forms of compliance. "We interpreted all pending situations as emergencies and signed immediately," Colvard noted in his diary. Even though the board had not put a clear stamp of approval on compliance, it still was a major breakthrough for the board and the state's publicly supported colleges and universities.

The board also authorized Colvard to establish or reestablish undergraduate courses at the Air Force base in Columbus. This was a relief to the MSU president because the university had received applications from two blacks for evening classes. "If we hold classes on the base, these students will be accommodated there. If we do not, they will likely be admitted on campus," Colvard noted in his diary in January 1965.

Integration appeared to be getting closer and closer to his office door, so Colvard, in his usual inimitable style, took the initiative. On February 9, 1965, he addressed the faculty and the students in separate meetings to lay out what he expected of them when integration came.

He started by recapping the pleasant events on campus, including MSU's first football victory against Ole Miss in seventeen years, and then he launched into his remarks about preparing for the future of integration.

He spoke about the Meredith situation at Ole Miss, opening the Graduate Record Examinations at MSU to all, although no black student had yet availed himself or herself of them, opening off-campus classes at Columbus Air Force base to all, and of his decision to sign the assurances of compliances to the Civil Rights Act of 1964. "Two or three things are clear, or at least I think they are clear," he continued. "One is that this institution cannot continue its present functions if its federal funds are cut off or are drastically reduced. A second is the fact that the legal machinery exists to bring about forced compliance with the Civil Rights Act of 1964. The third grows out of the other two: We have the choice of operating a first-class institution with federal funds or of operating a second- or fifth- or tenth-class institution without them; and either way the price to us ultimately is the same."

He explained that MSU and all other public institutions of higher learning in the state were bound by the same federal court order that forced the integration of Ole Miss in September 1962. "That changes are in the offing is evident," Colvard said. "We shall be called upon to do some things that we had rather not do. People who look toward Mississippi State may become divided. Our faculty and staff doubtless will not see things through a common eye. Students will have differing points of view. As we clear successive hurdles, we may not all be together in ideas or attitude, but we are and must be together in actuality when the chips are down. And they are beginning to get down. We face an evolution; it must not be a revolution. We must bend. We must not—being brittle—break. We must not—being too rigid—be broken. This institution must prevail, grow stronger, become increasingly excellent in performing its great work for our state and for its people. We simply must not fail."

MSU students and faculty have an opportunity to handle future problems in such a way that would be a refutation of many of the criticisms that Mississippi has incurred throughout the nation, he said. "The good people of Mississippi, whose literal sweat and toil have gone into the making of this institution, look this way in confidence," Colvard said. "The alumni believe in and back us in our mission. The students see their hope in Mississippi State. The progress and growth of our state is importantly related to the continued and increasing excellence of our effort. Mississippi State University—she simply must not fail or falter."

Immediately following his speech, the general faculty unanimously gave a vote of confidence to Colvard and the governing board. The campus newspaper published a story with the headline, "Colvard Calls for Good Judgment to Insure Future Growth of MSU." The *Starkville Daily News* published the speech in its entirety. "If there was any negative reaction in the community, it did not come to my attention," Colvard noted in *Mixed Emotions*. "Mississippi State University had been fortunate that through all these situations, we had no on-campus disturbances and no major internal disagreements. We were getting close to the next major step—that of admitting our first black students on the campus. We thought we had prepared ourselves for that about as well as we could."

6

THE TIME
HAS COME

The day that President Colvard knew would come sooner or later began quietly three weeks before the summer session was to start on July 19, 1965. As MSU registrar Lynn Ferguson went through the mail containing the latest batch of applications, he noticed that one stood out from the rest. The applicant, a college transfer student named Richard Holmes of Starkville, had graduated from Henderson High School in Starkville, an all-black school. It was a complete application, with the signatures of five MSU alumni attached.

Ferguson realized that, although there had been no lawsuit nor court order, MSU had indeed received its first black applicant, and he immediately notified Colvard's office. "One of the first things I did was to call Governor Paul Johnson," Colvard recalled. "He did not seem surprised and said, 'We must work together in handling these matters.' What a contrast from what might have been expected from former Governor Barnett." Colvard also informed the governing board and on June 25 sent out a news release and letter to the alumni asking for their cooperation in what he noted was sure to be a trying time. He did not name the applicant at the time and news coverage was minimal—only a four-paragraph story in the *Starkville News* with the single column headline, "Negro Will Enroll for MSU Session."

But Colvard was particularly anxious to secure the governor's cooperation. Although Johnson, standing in for Barnett at one point, also had defied federal authorities at Ole Miss when he was lieutenant governor, he had shown signs of softening his approach. During his inauguration address in January of 1964, Johnson made no reference to defending segregation, and Colvard had been encouraged. Invited as a special guest to the inaugural, Colvard reported in his diary that Johnson had said "he was governor of both Negro and white and that we are both Mississippians and Americans."

The conciliatory nature of Johnson's inaugural speech drew front-page coverage in the *New York Times* and coverage from *Time* magazine.

He had said, "I would point out to you that the Mississippi economy is not divisible by political party or faction, or even by race, color or creed. As of this hour, Paul Johnson is working for everybody with every resource at his command. I will say to you that you and I are part of this world, whether we like it or not. We are Americans as well as Mississippians. Hate or prejudice or ignorance will not lead Mississippi while I sit in the governor's chair." The *Time* article noted that Johnson concluded with, "God bless every one of you, all Mississippians, black and white, here and away from home."

The governor's patience was to be tested many times in the next few years as Freedom Riders came into the state, Freedom Schools were organized to teach blacks how to register to vote, sit-ins were held in several major Mississippi cities, and international attention was focused on the state after the murder of three civil rights workers. (Johnson did not waver from his somewhat enlightened stance, and he was defeated in his bid to become lieutenant governor in 1967. Mississippi governors could not succeed themselves.)

During Johnson's campaign in November 1963, someone from his office had called Colvard to squelch any rumors that he may have heard that Johnson intended to replace him as MSU president. A few months after he had been inaugurated, Johnson called Colvard into his office in Jackson for a conference on the future of higher education in Mississippi. Colvard interpreted that occasion as another positive sign, although progress was still agonizingly slow. "I must record that Paul Johnson has much greater capacity for leadership than Barnett," Colvard had written in his diary in late 1964. "Johnson has been very helpful and friendly with me." He had helped Colvard get a legislative appropriation to buy an abandoned textile factory adjoining the university as a maintenance-building headquarters for MSU.

Although the governor was friendly toward Colvard, he had been elected on a staunchly segregationist platform. Since Governor Barnett had praised him for standing tall against federal officials at Ole Miss,

Johnson adopted a campaign slogan, "Stand Tall with Paul." His campaign literature said: "Paul Johnson stood up for you and all the people of Mississippi. Now it's time for you to stand tall with Paul!" During the campaign, Johnson told a Harperville audience, "The Kennedys are out to put you flat on your back with the Negro's heel on your throat. We've got to get those Kennedys out of office. The focal issue of this campaign is whether the Kennedys will break the back of Mississippi, and southern resistance to federal encroachment. If I am defeated, you can be sure they will ram it down your throats." His campaign literature emphasized "our segregated way of life which is best for both races, now and forever! States rights, local self-government. In the crucial four years ahead, Mississippi needs a man unafraid to stand up and meet the serious challenges that are sure to come. Paul Johnson is that man! Stand up for Mississippi!"

As Colvard had been trying to get his faculty and students ready for integration, Richard Holmes had been watching and waiting. He was a twenty-one-year-old junior at the eight-hundred-student, all-black Wiley College, four hundred miles away in Marshall, Texas. His hope was to find a way to take summer classes closer to home. "It was not to integrate Mississippi State," he recalled years later in an interview with the MSU alumni magazine. His foster father, Dr. Douglas Conner, a prominent black physician in Starkville, had kept Holmes informed of Colvard's actions at MSU, including his bend-don't-break speech in February, which urged peaceful compliance to civil rights legislation.

"I asked myself why should I go to Alcorn or Jackson State or other places (all black colleges) when Mississippi State was in my hometown," Holmes recalled. "I had always thought of Starkville as an atypical Mississippi town and Mississippi State as an atypical Mississippi university. Starkville had always been a place of warm race relations for as long as I could remember, even when things in Mississippi and around the country seemed to be falling apart. I didn't perceive that the blacks or whites of Starkville or those at Mississippi State would have any adverse reaction to my attending State." He said that he had talked with white MSU students he knew in Starkville before making his decision and that one of them had even offered to lend him some of his textbooks. Conner recalled that he encouraged Holmes to enroll at MSU. "I had talked with various people and the consensus seemed to be that what had happened at Ole Miss wouldn't happen here," he told the alumni magazine. "There was some concern, but not much."

There was no lawsuit, no court order, and no advance publicity. Conner, who was president of the local NAACP (National Association for the Advancement of Colored People) chapter, but not considered an inflammatory civil rights activist, recalled, "It really was Richard's decision. He said that he wanted to get closer to home. He was doing very well at Wiley, but he just wanted to transfer to State. We told him that, in coming, he was not to go out (to campus) with a chip on his shoulder. Just keep his head up. If any untoward remarks were made, he should not say anything back, but should make a note of it if it had to be reported later."

In many ways, Holmes was a perfect candidate to be the first African American at MSU. Quiet, serious, and studious, he was not intent upon making history, but he was focused on becoming a doctor, like his brother and his foster father.

Holmes had been born in Chicago, but when he was only eighteen months old, he and three of his brothers were moved to Starkville to live with his grandmother, Mrs. Eliza Hunter. When she learned she was dying of cancer, Mrs. Hunter asked Conner, who was her doctor, to take care of Richard. Conner and his wife, the parents of two children, agreed to do so.

Holmes was only twelve when his grandmother died in 1956, but he credited her and Conner as the two most important motivators in his life. "Although she was uneducated," Holmes said of his grandmother, "she motivated my brothers and me. She helped raise four of the six boys in my family. Of the four, three went to professional or graduate schools and two of those got their Ph.D.s. Basically, she had three axioms: work hard, go to church, and stay in school. She had a tenacious respect for law and order, and she projected that to us." As for Conner, Holmes said, "He was probably my earliest inspiration to go into medicine. During my elementary and high school years, I worked at his office. First, I was a janitor, then eventually I helped with minor things in the lab. My interest in medicine more or less blossomed from the periphery."

On the day Holmes registered at MSU, July 19, 1965, Conner drove his foster son to the entrance of the Animal Husbandry Building, where registration was being held. "Keep your head up," he told him and drove away, leaving him as the only black face among hundreds of white students lining up to register. Colvard and his forces were ready and waiting as Holmes approached the registration site about 2:00

P.M. "While we had prepared both the community and the campus for this event as well as we could, we were not so naive as to believe that we had eliminated the possibilities that hotheaded and riotous reactions could develop under the leadership of some of those still adhering to the never, never doctrine," Colvard noted in *Mixed Emotions.*

But there were no state troopers or federal troops visible when Holmes got out of his foster father's car. There were no television camera crews or reporters of any kind in sight. (Colvard had arranged for Holmes to meet them at a press conference after registration.) As Colvard had hoped it would be, that Tuesday appeared to be just another normal day of registering a record 2,800 students for the summer session. Plainclothes officers were watching Holmes carefully, but from a distance as he finished registering for his two classes in psychology and American government and walked the short distance to the Lee Hall administration building to pay his fees of $93.33.

Holmes, who was wearing a light blue sports coat and a tie, did not attempt to speak with the students. As he waited in line at Lee Hall, he did not notice that Colvard had stepped out of his office down the hall to take a look at one of his new students. "He was just another student," Colvard recalled. "That was a very pleasing sight to behold." The MSU president and the first black student were not to meet until nearly thirty-eight years later. Both had been invited as special guests at a dinner in Starkville celebrating the 125th anniversary of the founding of Mississippi State. By this time, February 28, 2003, Colvard had long been retired, and Holmes had taken a job as a staff physician at Mississippi State's student health center. Photographers were on hand to record the long-awaited and cordial meeting that had not occurred in 1965.

After paying his fees with a check, Holmes had faced the press at the MSU media relations office in Lee Hall. He read a brief statement and answered questions in the session, which lasted only about fifteen minutes. "I realize that my entering Mississippi State University is a news item, and I know that the press and news media have a job to do," Holmes began reading from his statement. "But I hope that after today the press, news media, and the public will forget I am here. As a lifelong Mississippian, I am here to study and learn at a high-rated Mississippi university which just happens to be in my hometown. I seek no special favors and I hope that there will be no impediments from any source during my stay here at State."

In response to questions, he said, "I am not associated with the NAACP or any other group, and I have never been involved with civil rights demonstrations."

When someone asked if he intended to try out for football since he had played on the teams at Henderson High and Wiley, Holmes replied that he would not participate in any extracurricular activities, since he intended to live and eat at home in Starkville and commute to campus. The *Daily Times Leader* of nearby West Point reported, "The well-mannered, soft-spoken Negro answered all of the questions politely and stressed again that he entered State because of the 'closeness of the school to my home and its high rating.'" In response to another question, Holmes said, "There was no hostility shown me. I had no fear of registering here today, and I believe everything will continue to be as calm as it was today."

News coverage played the event as peaceful and orderly. Even the usually inflammatory Jackson *Clarion-Ledger* had a front-page headline that read, "No Incidents as MSU Registers First Negro." The lead paragraph in the Associated Press story from Starkville read: "Fellow students shook his hand and chattered freely with Negro Richard Holmes Monday as he walked onto the Mississippi State University campus to become the first of his race to register there." After waiting three days to see if any problems arose, Colvard finally took his family vacation. A month later he noted in his diary, "It appears that what was considered a major hurdle has turned out to be no problem. The University has gained stature."

Dr. Conner, Holmes's foster father, told the alumni magazine years later that on the night after Holmes had registered, a group of white students marched from the campus to surround his house shouting anti-integration slogans. "They didn't try to do anything to the house and we stayed inside and kept the outside lights on," Conner said. "After they had vented their spleen, they just marched back to campus. I'm sure all of them weren't students because I'm sure a lot of riff-raff got in the line, but it started on campus. We did call the police, but I waited a little while before doing so because I thought they might pass on by. They had dispersed, however, before the police arrived." Conner said there were no further incidents, although he did receive a few harassing phone calls.

Holmes said he had no problems during the summer term, but found it lonely at MSU and considered going back to Wiley where he had friends. "In talking with Dr. Conner and several members of the black community, I was asked to stay," Holmes recalled. "They felt that if I didn't no other black would enroll at Mississippi State. At the time, another black student in Starkville was thinking about coming, but he said he would not enroll if I wasn't there. So, in the fall, there were two black students at State."

Once the regular fall session started, Holmes said, some nasty words were hurled at him. "I heard a lot more catcalls," he said. "I met more resistance from the student body. A lot of it might have come from freshmen, but I really can't say because I didn't look around every time I heard an unpleasant word. Still, there were only verbal unpleasantries. No one pushed me or spat upon me or anything like that. As a whole, the students were relatively polite. Seldom did anyone go ahead of me through a door and slam it in my face. Usually they would just speak to me. Things that I heard were usually from across campus or across the way. No one directly approached me or abused me. When I was in the library, I could sit at a table and have the entire table to myself—which was interesting. But things like that were of no great consequence."

Colvard noted in his diary, "This marks the beginning of a new era at MSU, an era that is past due but one that could release our people from their own prejudices and allow a degree of greatness to emerge."

Holmes went on to receive his bachelor's and master's degrees from MSU and then went on to medical school at Michigan State University, graduating in 1977. He had promised himself that he would return to practice medicine in Mississippi, so after interning and completing residency requirements in Tuscaloosa, Alabama; Toledo, Ohio; and Alabaster, Alabama, he opened a family and emergency medicine practice in 1981 in Columbus.

"Mississippi has great potential and there's a lot of work that needs to be done in medicine, education, and economics," Holmes told the MSU alumni magazine in a 1982 interview. "Sure there's some resistance still to be overcome here in the South, but, basically having lived in Michigan and Ohio, we have found that people are more genuine here; they are friendlier and more honest. I had rather live among people like that. Here in the South, you generally know how people feel about you. I think blacks have an equal chance of doing well here in Mississippi, as in any area of the country. But this is home. If you are going to take a stand or make an impression, why not here?"

After Colvard breathed a giant sigh of relief following Holmes's first days at MSU, he and his family left for a vacation on the North Carolina shore. While he was there, he was contacted again by the University of North Carolina about the possible chancellorship of a new branch at Charlotte. He let the North Carolina folks know he was still interested, if such a position opened up. "It is impossible for me to know how I would have performed had the first black appeared at Mississippi State instead of Ole Miss in face of the strong resistance generated by Governor Barnett," Colvard wrote in *Mixed Emotions*. "I am sure my objectives would have been the same as when Richard Holmes did come to Mississippi State, but I am equally sure my strategy would have been quite different from the one we followed at a later time and under different circumstances. The reality was that we dealt with our problems as they developed, and we prepared for the inevitable."

The Colvards returned to Starkville on August 6, and Colvard began preparing for the fall semester. "There has been absolutely no incident resulting from the enrollment of our first Negro," he wrote in his diary. "He has conducted himself very well. He and at least one—perhaps three or four—other Negroes will enroll in September."

Meanwhile, the MSU Foundation's Patrons of Excellence program continued to pick up momentum. A banquet was being planned for October 8 to honor sixty-four members who had pledged at least $10,000 each. "When I was introduced they gave me a rising ovation," Colvard noted in his diary. "This group has been wonderful in helping us to get our development program underway."

The principal uses of the foundation money were for scholarships, supplements to faculty salaries, and occasionally the construction of buildings, such as the Chapel of Memories and carillon tower. The chapel was built with the bricks remaining from Old Main dormitory after it burned, and with new bricks given by an alumnus and $10,000 contributed by five patrons. State Senator Ben Frank Hilbun, son of former MSU President Ben Hilbun, was a member of the State Building Commission. Old Main had burned during the last months of the Hilbun presidency. The president had proposed the building of a chapel as a memorial to Old Main. His son had persuaded the Building Commission to add $30,000 to the other funds available to build the chapel. The carillon and tower were given by another alumnus and his wife who had become Patrons of Excellence.

While Colvard continued working hard on MSU business, University of North Carolina system officials were putting the finishing touches on creating a new branch at Charlotte and keeping Colvard informed that he was the prime candidate to be chancellor. Finally, on Saturday morning, October 23, UNC system president William Friday called Colvard and said the selection committee had voted unanimously to offer him the job, although there were still some details that had to be settled before it could be made firm. Colvard said he was very interested, but he would need some time to inform his governing board. He wrote in his diary, "Barring unexpected developments I guess this about ends a long period, 15 months, of indecision on that situation."

While he was waiting for Friday to call back, Colvard received two unsolicited calls, one from a University of Missouri representative informing him that his name had been put on the short list for the presidency of that institution and another from an Oklahoma State University official saying the selection committee there wanted to talk to him about possibly becoming OSU president. "I hope I am worthy of this rather extensive consideration," Colvard wrote in his diary. "Somehow I feel that I'm overrated."

Colvard concluded that one reason he was being considered for top posts at several locations might be because he had been giving speeches on the importance and principles of good administration in higher education. "I had decided that because of the way my career was developing I would never be able to get back to academic research, so I decided that I would devote my attention to studying the principles of administration," Colvard said. He read and studied extensively and put together a speech titled "What Is Good Administration?" that he delivered for the first time in July 1962 at a national meeting of deans of agriculture of land-grant colleges and universities in Lincoln, Nebraska. It was a strong, insightful presentation that caught the attention of other college and university administrators all across the country. After that appearance, he was asked to deliver the same speech at various conferences.

"Few, if any, of us who have been given administrative assignments in colleges and universities have been trained for our jobs," Colvard said. "In the world of business, an administrator deals with groups of people of similar or closely related talents all working together toward a centrally controlled objective of something to be produced or sold. An educational administrator, on the other hand, must mobilize a multiplicity of talents from all sorts and conditions of staff and somehow achieve some rather clearly defined institutional objectives. The very essence of a university is its diversity—a diversity which must present at least a semblance of unity to public view. So, the administrator may have to be a magician, indeed."

He laid out seven essentials of good administration, such as the practice of consultation, and explained the value of each. "The administrator's task is not an easy one," he said. "He must know everything that is going on but not masquerade as a know-it-all. He must have a finger on everything but not in everything. He must know how far to go and how far not to go. And rest assured, that whatever happens, the administrator stands to be damned if he does and damned if he doesn't—and perhaps most successful administrators when faced with the choice, choose to be damned for doing. If he is unusually successful in mobilizing the intellectual resources of his campus and is so fortunate as to have or is able to attract associates of high competency, there is no end to what can be accomplished."

On Friday, November 25, 1965, the MSU Development Foundation board of directors met and reported assets had reached more than $1 million.

In December, Colvard continued to meet with representatives of Missouri and Oklahoma State and tried to get a definitive answer from UNC.

"I really do not want to leave," he wrote in his diary, "but the top leadership here is neither encouraging nor inspiring. . . . the principal challenge at Charlotte has from the beginning been the opportunity to help build a new university." He also expressed his high regard for President William Friday, who would be his boss and was largely responsible for the new connection.

Finally, North Carolina got its act in order and extended a solid offer to Colvard to become the first chancellor of the new university in the state's largest city, Charlotte. He accepted on January 23, 1966, with an effective date of March 1. In his typical analytical fashion, Colvard listed the positives and negatives of his move in his diary on February 18. "We are leaving a well organized and comparatively stable university to go to a fledgling institution," he wrote. "We are giving up personal comforts and perquisites such as a good home—well maintained, laundry, servants and low costs for entertaining." He noted that he saw a great challenge in helping build a new university, "greater than that provided by heading larger and more mature institutions."

He listed seven negatives and seventeen positives, ending, "Mississippi State University is well organized and faces no major crisis at this time. It may be a good time to leave. I have stayed through some of the most difficult years. Integration problems have been met and solved."

Colvard's decision was a bitter blow to many connected with MSU, and not all reaction was positive. After his decision became public, Colvard was told that somebody had said, "Well, now we can get a president of our own." The Development Foundation officers immediately beseeched him to change his mind, but to no avail. That was when one even promised to raise money for a Colvard for Governor campaign, if he would stay in Mississippi. Colvard said he appreciated the vote of confidence, but running for governor was the last thing on his mind.

But he could look back on his tenure at Mississippi State with pride. "During the Colvard Years the faculty turnover was consistently less than 10 percent annually. This in the face of the national image of Mississippi, which had been marred by civil rights activity and an unfavorable national press," his successor, Dr. William L. Giles, reported at the end of the 1965–66 academic year. "Faculty salaries increased. The size of the student body grew from 4,725 to 7,305. The physical plant expanded." Giles, an Oklahoma native who had received his Ph.D. at the University of Missouri, had been superintendent of MSU's Delta Branch Experiment Station when Colvard convinced him to become MSU vice president for agriculture and forestry. Giles listed the major projects accomplished on Colvard's watch: new faculty dwellings, the Walker Engineering Building, the Horticulture Teaching Laboratory, the Raspet Flight Laboratory, the Dorris Ballew Animal Science Building, the Hand Chemical Laboratories, Cresswell Hall, the Union, the Student Health Center, Evans Hall, and the Chapel of Memories. Giles paid high tribute to his predecessor: "The image of the man reflected the image of the institution, and Mississippi State University gained stature under his leadership and the very solid support from groups throughout the state." Colvard was pleased that Giles had become his successor, because his selection indicated that the team Colvard had put together would continue to lead MSU. "In most instances the selection of a university president is a long and drawn-out process requiring many months and often the appointment of acting presidents while the decision is being made," Colvard recalled. "This can create uncertainty and periods of disruption among faculties." So Colvard was happy when three of his top officers told him they wanted to stay together as a team and asked him to discourage any groups from promoting one over the other. Colvard called faculty leaders and assured them that if any one of the three were selected, he would have the support of the others. "This, in effect, left my leadership team in charge and assured trustees that prompt action could be taken without risking damaging internal dissension. Thus it was possible for me to introduce my successor to the faculty before my departure."

Colvard received dozens of congratulatory letters. One he treasured came from his old nemesis M. M. Roberts. "You and I never had but one real difference and that had to do with athletics; but that is out of my life now and I hope it is out of yours," Roberts wrote. "Under your leadership, Mississippi State University has grown greatly in the minds of educators about us and also in the minds of Mississippians which the University serves so wonderfully well. We are grateful to you for the part you played in this segment of university life there."

Black educator C. C. Mosley, director of graduate studies at Jackson State College in Jackson, wrote, "I have watched the growth of Mississippi State University and I know some of the gigantic problems that faced you as president of the university. . . . The method in which you handled these problems gained my highest respect for you." Alumnus James B. Puryear of Tallahassee, Florida, wrote, "Having brought Mississippi State through the most difficult time of its history, you have strengthened it and given it added life. Your strong, positive leadership was constantly evident, and it was inspiring to me, personally, to see a man willing to assert his beliefs and stick by them." Mississippi state treasurer William Winter, who later became governor, wrote, "I am glad that we had the opportunity for your leadership during the particular crucial years which you were here, and your influence will be felt for a long time to come. You helped get us by some critical decisions and the state is better for your having been here."

Colvard was pleased with his record at MSU and felt he was leaving the university in good hands. "Most of all I was proud that what I had identified as an inferiority complex seemed to have been replaced with pride and positive expectations."

A few months later, in late 1967, the new governor, Paul Johnson, made a speech to business leaders in Los Angeles saying, "Mississippi has survived. She has conquered adversity. She disdains mediocrity. She will attain excellence." The newspaper in Aberdeen, Mississippi, picked up the quote and continued in an editorial, "The term 'Striving for Excellence' was first put into general use in the state by Dr. Dean Colvard, then president of Mississippi State University. It is to Governor Johnson's credit that he recognizes the outstanding no matter its source." Colvard was encouraged that the statement gave at least a glimmer of hope that leadership in the state was changing.

Dean Colvard (left) and Dr. Richard Holmes (center), first black student at Mississippi State University, with new President, Charles Lee, February 28, 2003. Courtesy of Mississippi State University Foundation.

Colvard family portrait, 1960.

1963 MSU basketball team. Courtesy of Mississippi State University Foundation.

1963 MSU Basketball Coach Babe McCarthy.
Courtesy of Mississippi State University
Foundation.

Wallace, Martha, and Dean Colvard vacation on the Gulf Coast of Mississippi, 1964. Courtesy of Mississippi State University Foundation.

Charles S. Whittington (seated, left), president of the corporation, signs the charter for the MSU Development Foundation on February 4, 1962, as MSU President Dean Colvard (seated, center) and Louis C. Spencer, Jr., look on. Standing (from left) are W. B. Donald, H. E. Allen, and J. C. Redd. Foundation officers not pictured were Lewis F. Mallory, Dr. T. K. Martin, Dorris Ballew, George Perry, T. E. Case, and H. B. Crosby. Courtesy of Mississippi State University Foundation.

Martha and Dean Colvard at Colvard Union, Mississippi State University.

MSU President Dean Colvard (left) accepts the newly incorporated Development Foundation's first major commitment of property from Mr. and Mrs. Floyd Campbell White. The couple deeded 1.031 acres of land valued at $250,000 to the university and received benefits through a life estate in the property. Courtesy of Mississippi State University Foundation.

PART 2

7 A CHANCE TO BUILD A NEW UNIVERSITY

UNC President Bill Friday had personally recruited Dean Colvard to become the first chancellor of a new University of North Carolina at Charlotte. It was to be a complete university on the same status as the three others in existence at the time in Chapel Hill, Raleigh, and Greensboro. As such, the new institution needed an experienced leader, and preferably one with an earned doctorate degree. Friday could have his pick of any number of qualified candidates from across the nation for the new job in North Carolina's largest city. He recalled that he had considered several potential candidates, but he contacted only Colvard. "There were others, but he was the one I went after," Friday said.

He had first worked with Colvard when Colvard was dean of agriculture at NC State and Friday was assistant to UNC system president Gordon Gray. Their friendship continued when Friday succeeded Gray in 1956 and even after Colvard left NC State to become president of Mississippi State University in 1960. Characteristically, Friday, who was an NC State graduate as well as a UNC law-school alumnus, had kept in contact with Colvard. They served on similar committees of national organizations concerning higher education.

Friday first asked Colvard about the Charlotte job in July 1964, tracking him down when he was on vacation with his family at Carolina Beach near Wilmington. Colvard told him he wasn't looking for a job, but he would be interested in talking more about the Charlotte possibility. On August 12, 1964, they met in person, this time when they were among seventy-five state university presidents invited to have lunch with President Johnson in the White House to hear his proposals on how to fight poverty in America. They met again on December 11 of that year when Colvard flew to Raleigh for a meeting of the advisory board of the Agriculture Policy Institute, of which he was a member. On June 18, 1965, they met in Washington as members of a national ad hoc committee to find ways to help the predominantly minority colleges survive. Discussions between Colvard and Friday continued over the next several months while Colvard decided what to do. He could have stayed at MSU, and he was offered or considered for the presidency of several universities, including Auburn, Florida State, Oklahoma State, and even his alma mater, Berea College.

Finally, Friday called Colvard in Starkville on January 22, 1966, with a firm offer to come to Charlotte as the new university's first chancellor. His salary would be $27,000 per year and he would receive a $2,700 annual housing allowance plus moving expenses.

Colvard and his wife drove to Raleigh for an interview with the trustee committee and Governor Dan Moore, who was by law, chairman of the board. It was 1,443 miles round trip. The expense account that he submitted to Friday's office for reimbursement totaled $202.19, including mileage at eight cents per mile.

When word got out that Colvard had decided to accept the offer to go to Charlotte, his supporters at Mississippi State pledged support for his continuing as president there. The chairman of the board of directors of the university's foundation gave him a check for $5,000 to supplement his salary and offered him a new Cadillac automobile. Later the ante was upped to $10,000 per year as a supplement, but Colvard turned it down.

Colvard reported for work in Charlotte on April 1, 1966. "I had complete confidence in a great president, William Friday, who was widely respected for educational statesmanship," Colvard wrote in his diary at the time. "I had worked with him before. Anticipation of that renewed relationship had influenced my decision to undertake the new challenge."

In other developments, the university's first urban affairs forum, called "The University and the Development of the Modern City," one which Colvard had engineered even before taking over in Charlotte, had been a big hit in the spring of 1966, kicked off by Governor Dan K. Moore himself. In addition, Colvard reenergized the Foundation of the University of North Carolina at Charlotte with Charlotte banker

Addison Reese as chairman, and together they launched a Founding Patrons of Excellence Program that in less than a year had signed up ninety-five individuals or companies who pledged a minimum of $10,000 each over a ten-year period. He also had been successful in other efforts to recruit additional young and highly qualified faculty.

"There is great challenge in trying to put a new university together," Colvard wrote in his diary. "The advantages here over Miss State include 1. Many more cultural advantages 2. More association with successful and public-spirited people 3. Living in a state with a better reputation in politics, education and economics here. 4. A better place to spend the rest of one's life. 5. Stimulating experiences in urban life, in new aspects of education, such as the arts—this adds up to breadth of experience. Some disadvantages are 1. A smaller, less mature organization which requires more personal involvement in details 2. Loss of comforts of home and perquisites 3. Loss in net cash savings 4. Restrictive budget controls—had more freedom to manage in Miss."

He even found his relationship with the college's founder, Bonnie Cone, to be working out well. Initially, Cone's supporters had fought hard to have her designated as UNCC's first chancellor, but Friday and others in command realized that the new university would need someone with at least a Ph.D. and experience in having led a large institution, qualifications Cone did not have. She seemed to be satisfied with having been named vice chancellor under Colvard. "Bonnie and I bonded pretty well," Colvard recalled. "Bonnie was very good with students. She loved the students and the students loved her, but she was not a delegator. She couldn't turn loose. Her strength was community relations. She built the Friends of the University up to 400 or 500 members very quickly."

Of course, Colvard had not been around when Charlotte became the fourth campus of UNC. Bonnie Cone had been the insistent and persistent mother hen since 1946. Starting as a part-time teacher at a junior college for returning veterans of World War II, Cone became the Charlotte College Center's director in 1947 at the age of forty. She was the power behind the legislature's decision to create Charlotte College on April 4, 1949, as a junior college. She became president in 1961 when the campus, still just a junior college, had 915 students, although it had been moved from downtown Charlotte to a permanent site nine miles north of town.

The college had been upgraded to educate third-year students in

1963 and fourth-years in 1964, with Cone working diligently behind the scenes to woo Charlotte business leaders and legislators for support. Many people in Charlotte knew that making Charlotte College into a legitimate university consumed "Miss Bonnie." She often worked eighteen-hour days and pushed her staff to follow her example. She recruited faculty members from all over, enticing them with dreams of expansion. It was widely assumed that she would become the leader if and when university status was achieved. But because of her dedication to Charlotte College, she never went on to work toward a doctorate, a requirement that barred the way toward chancellor status.

Two weeks after arriving in Charlotte, Colvard left on a whirlwind tour of urban universities in Michigan, Illinois, and Missouri, using money Friday had found somehow in his budget. Colvard and Friday's assistant, Dr. Arnold King, visited Oakland University at Rochester, Michigan, which had recently been established as a branch of Michigan State. Then they flew to Chicago for a look at the Chicago Circle campus of the University of Illinois. This visit was followed by one to the Edwardsville campus of the University of Southern Illinois. The University of Missouri's St. Louis campus was the last stop. "In all of these studies, I sorted out the programs which would have greatest application in Charlotte," Colvard noted in his diary. "Vast differences between these emerging urban institutions and the well-established land-grant institutions, with which I had spent most of my career, reminded me that I had much to learn. This is a new and dynamic movement in higher education in this country. It provides an exciting opportunity to relate the university to current developments in society."

Within a few days of arriving in Charlotte, Colvard was off to Chapel Hill for a meeting of the administrative council of the consolidated university where he encountered his first foretelling of the problems that East Carolina College would likely be causing to draw attention, and possibly funds, away from UNCC. "I'm afraid the university is about to take the wrong position on East Carolina College," Colvard wrote in his diary. "They are destined to become a university and I hate to see President Friday and the rest of us fight a losing battle. I left feeling that perhaps a mistake was made in not joining with them in their efforts to make that campus a university. It was obvious, however, that President Leo Jenkins wanted it to be parallel rather than subordinate to the university system."

Jenkins had thrown down the gauntlet in a November 19, 1965, speech that left no doubt that the powerful political forces of the eastern part of the state were determined to have East Carolina become a full university, independent of the state system based in Chapel Hill with its campuses in Chapel Hill, Raleigh, Greensboro, and now Charlotte. "The East still lags behind the rest of the state because of the influence of Piedmont-centered universities which cannot possibly extend in undiminished strength into the East," Jenkins said in the speech at the Faculty Club of NC State. "The East needs its own university. . . . The people of Eastern North Carolina proudly look to East Carolina College, the state's third largest and fastest growing public institution, already organized into six schools, and they say, 'Here already stands a university. Why not then declare it so?'"

Jenkins did not have in mind that East Carolina should come into the consolidated university system as Charlotte College had done. As Mary Jo Jackson Bratton wrote in ECU's official history in 1986, "East Carolina supporters felt it was the essence of condescension to suggest that the third largest educational institution in the state, which operated a complete graduate program at the master's level, and whose five professional schools were fully accredited by their respective national and regional agencies, might in time merit the same approval that had been so handily extended to a small emergent institution that was still operating under only junior college accreditation."

While Jenkins continued to lobby hard in Raleigh for East Carolina, Colvard began putting together his new team at Charlotte. He had inherited a few experienced professors left over from Charlotte College, but he needed many new ones, and especially a right-hand man, a strong person with a solid background in academic administration, to put together a faculty. Most of the new hires would be young and untested, because Charlotte had no track record and low salaries compared to more prestigious institutions. "I felt I needed a good arts and sciences partner," Colvard said. "I needed to move quickly. The man we had was not very satisfactory to me. He had a very low boiling point. He was brilliant, almost a photographic memory, but he had sometimes challenged faculty members to go outside the door for a duel during a meeting. I was convinced that he could not be my right-hand man. I had to limp along with him until I could figure a way to make the transition."

Colvard called a friend of his at Emory University, Jock Ward, and others for recommendations. "I was repeatedly told that the man I was describing—the man I needed—was Hugh McEniry, for fifteen years Dean of Stetson University and former President of the Southern Association of Colleges and Schools," Colvard wrote later. "Usually the person making such a recommendation would conclude his comments by saying, 'but he would not be available.' I had never met him."

McEniry, who was fifty years old at the time, had spent twenty-seven years at Stetson in DeLand, Florida, fifteen of those years as dean. A graduate of Birmingham Southern College, he had received his M.A. and Ph.D. at Vanderbilt University. A stocky, substantial-looking man with a shock of white hair, black-framed glasses, and a ready smile, McEniry was considered the epitome of an academic administrator. He loved books and scholarship and relished spending hours discussing them.

Colvard tried to recruit McEniry by telephone, but McEniry told him he was not ready to leave Stetson. "It seemed that the major reason was that he was in a conflict of some sort with some of the leaders of the Baptist Church, which gave much support to Stetson, and that he did not want to leave until that conflict was resolved," Colvard said. "So we simply set the matter aside for a while and I continued to look. The more I looked, the more convinced I became that Hugh McEniry was the man we needed." So in November 1966, Colvard met McEniry in person in Miami, Florida, where both were attending the annual meeting of the Southern Association of Colleges and Schools. Colvard and Bonnie Cone then interviewed him. "I told him how exciting it was to be building a new university," Colvard said.

This time McEniry agreed to come to Charlotte for a visit. The university paid the travel expenses for McEniry and his wife from De-Land, but there was no money in the lean budget for entertainment, so Colvard prevailed upon the Higher Education Committee of the Charlotte Chamber of Commerce to host a dinner for the McEnirys at the Charlotte City Club. He also arranged for several community leaders to be present to help impress the McEnirys and convince them that they were needed and wanted. One of the guests was on the Wake Forest board and asked for and was granted the privilege of interviewing McEniry for the Wake Forest presidency.

A visit to the campus followed and Colvard popped the question again. This time McEniry agreed to come to UNCC. McEniry was not interested in pursuing the Wake Forest position, so he was to report to work in Charlotte on July 1, 1967, but Colvard soon found he had another problem—somehow the money to pay for his new vice chancellor of academic affairs had been left out of the state budget. Colvard was shocked and embarrassed. "I had been working on this matter for months with the knowledge of all concerned and had finally achieved what appeared to be the first significant breakthrough on personnel and a major goal toward building a university, only to be told that the position was not allowed," he recalled.

While he was with President Friday in Friday's office at Chapel Hill, Colvard received his permission to make a phone call to Governor Dan Moore's office. He reached Moore's administrative assistant, Ed Rankin, and asked to speak to the governor to see if there was a way to remedy the situation. Rankin told him Moore was out of the state. Colvard then said, "I asked to talk with him wherever he was and added that I would consider calling a press conference and resigning, stating the reasons, before I would go back on the proposition which had been so many months in coming into fruition." At this point, Rankin and Friday came up with the solution—the university would simply upgrade the salary of the acting dean of the faculty sufficiently to handle the situation. McEniry reported as planned in July 1967 and quickly became Colvard's invaluable assistant. He was present for Colvard's installation. "I felt very free in delegating responsibilities to him," Colvard recalled. "I took him in as a full partner. I trusted him completely and shared information without reservation. He was more or less the educational philosopher of the campus." Colvard noted in his diary on September 8, 1967, "I'm convinced that he is the best man in the country for this particular assignment. His coming was a milestone for UNCC. They will need me less from now on."

The discovery that McEniry's position was unfunded was followed by disclosure that no money had been appropriated for any of the five top leader positions he had sought from the 1967 legislature. "That was when we decided that we would have to seek planning funds elsewhere," Colvard recalled later.

He and McEniry worked so well together that they never disagreed on major items. "We had an understanding that we would not permit dissident individuals or groups to split us apart, that we would confer freely and often and stand together on major decisions. This we did," Colvard recalled.

Later he wrote, "With Hugh McEniry on our team I could spend more time with other phases of development. I turned the academic program over to him and sought his counsel on many other matters." McEniry was to stay as Colvard's right-hand man for six years. He and his wife, Mary, bought a seventeen-acre tract near Huntersville and dubbed it "Rural Simplicity." They built a lake, stocked it with fish,

and invited friends often to come and try their luck. They always culti-
vated a huge vegetable garden.

With his chief academic assistant finally in the fold, Colvard turned
to the other many tasks involved in building the new campus. He continued to recruit new faculty members, court Charlotte business leaders, and conduct the various aspects of his busy job as the smolder-
ing East Carolina situation continued to heat up. At one point, both
the water wells at the new Charlotte campus dried up at once. "We
couldn't even flush the toilets," Colvard recalled. He immediately ordered water brought in by tanker trucks until new wells could be drilled,
but he knew that was only temporary. He called Charlotte Mayor Stan
Brookshire and Mecklenburg County Commission Chairman Jim Martin (later North Carolina governor and then U.S. representative) for
help in pushing a planned water line construction as soon as possible.
"Sewer was almost as critical," Colvard said. "We activated sewage service one day before students were to move into our first dormitory. We
had to lay boards across the mud for them to walk across."

The fact that there was a buyer's market for professors during the
time Colvard was staffing the new university worked in his favor. Nationally, college and university enrollments were level or in decline, so
when positions were advertised in the *Chronicle of Higher Education* and
other higher education journals, the response was often overwhelming. It was common to receive more than one hundred applications for
a single opening. The fortunate result for Colvard was that the infant
university was able to attract the brightest from the beginning. Young
men and women who during fatter times would surely have landed on
the campuses of "big-name" institutions such as Stanford, Duke, and
Chapel Hill wound up at UNCC. The downside was that they generally
had little experience outside their own alma maters, and they tended
to think that the new, unformed academic outpost in Charlotte should
be colonized in the order of whatever institution they had recently
vacated. Despite that handicap, they were brimming with ideas and
eager to see things change. That was what excited Colvard. He wanted
to insure that those ideas were exposed and debated and that the best
ones would be implemented. He wanted creativity to bubble up from
every corner of the university. He wanted those young minds to have
an impact on the new institution and, through it, on society.

If he had learned anything from his years at NCSU and MSU, it was
the value of the team in getting things done. First, there had to be strong

senior leadership to steady the boat. Then, every level from there on down had to be brought on board. So in a proposal submitted in April 1968 to the Z. Smith Reynolds and Mary Reynolds Babcock Foundations, Colvard summed it up this way: "The need is for a major planning effort, one which will guarantee maximum results from the state's commitment. The mood of the faculty is to be innovative, to take some risks, and to establish the institution on the basis of contemporary needs and contemporary thought. The plea which is made by this proposal is for the privilege of engaging the best minds the country has to offer in the planning process and to take certain steps in early implementation which will add spirit and tone to the life of an emerging university."

Everywhere he had been, his administrative style had been defined by this bedrock principle: identify the problems and issues, bring in the best minds available, and then, "Let 'em rack!" (a favorite Colvard encouragement denoting an equestrian term to let the horse run at full gallop). He did not abandon this approach in the planning of UNC Charlotte. Indeed he went on to explain to the two foundations that "the procedure . . . would involve: (1) the designation of specific areas to be studied; (2) the selection of a competent educator as leader; (3) provision for members of the University faculty to visit and study other institutions known to be involved in innovative planning; (4) inviting to the campus from four to six top leaders in each designated area for a period of two days for the purpose of bringing about interactions with faculty members and with their counterparts on other campuses of the University; and (5) a careful synthesis and analysis of the various alternatives presented."

In all, seventy top leaders were brought in to advise and consult in seventeen areas. Most of the leaders came from academia, but others were invited from the media, financial institutions, and professional associations. (A complete list of the leaders and their affiliations is included in the appendix.)

Bright, unfettered minds were brought into direct contact with excellent leadership and experience. Work was focused on clearly defined issues and subjected to wide-open debate and exchange. True to his own roots, he called the approach the "organic process" and would later concede, even through his modesty, that it was one of his lasting contributions. The outcome literally shaped the institution forever, lasting through successive changes in faculty and administration.

In his report to the Reynolds Foundations, "Emergence of a University," Colvard included reaction from some of the visiting consultants after their visits to UNCC during the planning process.

For instance, Dr. James B. Pearson, professor of history at the University of Texas, wrote, "The visit to your campus was a most pleasant and stimulating experience—I only wish that our entire faculty could be so completely involved in planning the future of the University of Texas." Dr. Henry Freiser, chemistry professor at the University of Arizona, commented, "It seems to me that what took place was an almost ideal barrier-free communication experience, with the interchange of ideas and points of view between UNCC administrators, faculty, visitors and consultants occurring with unusual freedom." And Dr. Richard S. Dunn, history professor at the University of Michigan, said, "Everyone I talked to, from the Chancellor to the most junior faculty member, wants a quality graduate program which will strengthen the institution and help the community. UNCC, because it is still relatively small and young, has a marvelous opportunity to escape past mistakes and traditions in designing its graduate educational program."

8

A PROBLEM ARISES
IN THE EAST

Thirty-four-year-old Leo Jenkins had arrived in 1947 as a new dean on the campus of East Carolina Teachers College in Greenville fresh from serving as assistant to the commissioner of higher education in New Jersey. A native of Elizabeth, New Jersey, Jenkins had received his bachelor's degree from Rutgers, his master's from Columbia, and his doctorate in education from New York University before entering the Marine Corps in World War II. He fought on Guam and Iwo Jima and was awarded a Bronze Star for heroism. After his discharge at the end of the war, he returned to New Jersey, where he was hired as an instructor in political science at New Jersey State Teachers College.

Jenkins took the job at East Carolina planning to stay only a year or two, but he soon became a protégé of the college's president, the handsome, charismatic Dr. John D. Messick, who began grooming Jenkins to take over for him when Messick retired in 1960. Jenkins and Messick had become friends at New Jersey State when Messick was assistant to the president before leaving in 1947 to become president at East Carolina, taking Jenkins with him.

Just before his retirement, Messick strongly endorsed Jenkins to become his successor. The board of trustees agreed, and Jenkins took over at the age of forty-six in January 1960, during the same time Colvard was signing up for the Mississippi State job. Jenkins quickly let everyone know that he had grand plans for East Carolina. On the day of his appointment, he obtained approval from the trustees to seek state permission to add a master's degree in business administration to the curriculum. At the time of his inauguration in May 1960, Jenkins presided over a student body of 4,500. There was no UNC Charlotte; Charlotte College was simply a community college with fewer than 900 students.

Encouraged by leaders in the region, Jenkins was convinced that East Carolina should become the catalyst for economic growth in all of eastern North Carolina. Immediately after his selection as president, he sought approval from the state Board of Higher Education for a School of Nursing, which was permitted, but his push for an MBA program was denied. Nevertheless, he kept the pressure on until it was finally approved in 1966.

Jenkins, who was the father of six children, was a Renaissance man. He was an accomplished painter and lover of the arts. Under his command, East Carolina moved into serious programs in art, music, drama, and literature. At the same time, he pushed for a research and development institute and a strong athletics program, including the college's acceptance into the Southern Conference, after a decade of trying, and even a rowing team, which practiced on the Tar River in used sculls that had been donated by eastern universities.

Located about eighty-five miles east of the state capital of Raleigh, East Carolina's home campus in Greenville was in the center of a twenty-two-county region dotted with little more than tobacco farms and pig farms stretching fifty-five miles east of Greenville to the Atlantic Coast, where fishing was king and tourism was just beginning to emerge as a major industry. The region was poorer than the rest of the state and had virtually been overlooked by industry and major business, most of which was located in what was known as a Piedmont Crescent, stretching from Raleigh along Interstate 85 to Charlotte, 120 miles south.

Jenkins's ambitions appeared to know no bounds, as educators in Charlotte and other areas of the state learned. In July 1964, he had even told the North Carolina General Assembly's Advisory Budget Committee on its visit to Greenville that he would seek approval for a two-year medical school. This proposal brought stiff opposition from leaders in Charlotte and in Chapel Hill, but Jenkins was undaunted. His plans received a major boost in October of that year when the East Carolina board of trustees elected thirty-eight-year-old alumnus Robert B. Morgan as chairman. An engaging and forceful personality, Morgan was serving his third term in the state senate, having been elected first at the age of twenty-nine. Amazingly he already had five years of public service at that point, since he had been elected Harnett County clerk of court in 1950 at the age of twenty-four while he was still in law school at Wake Forest University. Morgan was a close ally of the powerful I. Beverly Lake, an influential Raleigh lawyer who had run for governor in 1960, losing to Terry Sanford. Morgan was the campaign manager for Lake, his old law professor at Wake Forest. Although Lake lost the statewide vote, he carried nearly every county in eastern North Carolina, proving his popularity there, with Morgan on his coattails. But by 1960 Morgan had begun to forge his own political career, and later he became the state's attorney general and then a U.S. Senator.

In 1964 Morgan turned his attention to helping Leo Jenkins make East Carolina into a full-fledged university, one independent of the consolidated University of North Carolina with its campuses in Raleigh, Greensboro, and Chapel Hill. They would start with the two-year medical school and then move up the ladder. Other political leaders in the region joined with Morgan to make a powerful bloc of votes in the state house and senate, one that the governor and other power brokers would have to reckon with if they wanted anything of value accomplished.

Arguing for the two-year med school, Jenkins and Morgan pointed out that eastern North Carolina had fewer than 50 physicians per 100,000 population, although the state's average was 75 and the nation's 125. The region also suffered from the highest infant mortality rate in the country. Jenkins noted that only 115 North Carolina students were admitted to the three medical schools in the state in 1963 and only 24 gained admission to medical schools out of the state. Other leaders in the medical community throughout the state agreed that North Carolina needed more trained physicians. Jenkins and Morgan launched a series of speaking engagements, addressing civic clubs, church groups, anybody who would listen. In April, eastern legislators introduced bills in the state house and senate to establish the medical school. In May, a special state medical center study commission recommended against it, but in July the legislature authorized its establishment.

Jenkins, Morgan, and their followers were jubilant. They had taken on UNC and its followers and had won. The success was duly noted across the state. The *Raleigh Times* noted, "Such a school would, without doubt, launch East Carolina toward university status, with a venture which would be as costly as it would be ambitious."

At the same March 1965 session the North Carolina legislature was allowing the creation of the two-year medical school at East Carolina, it approved expansion of the three-campus UNC system to take in its fourth campus, the University of North Carolina at Charlotte. A glance backward showed that Colvard's friend and mentor, Bill Friday, president of the consolidated UNC system and architect of its expansion, may have underestimated Jenkins's chances of success in ever getting East Carolina classified as a full-fledged university. Jenkins and his supporters insisted that the call for independent university status for ECC in the legislature was not a ploy to get it admitted as another branch of UNC. That would only mean more fetters and restrictions. Then on March 8, 1967, a bill was introduced in the state senate to make ECC an independent university.

Former governor Luther Hodges testified during hearings on the bill, "We must prevent the building of empires on the part of any college president or board which might be jealous of other colleges and, in particular, of the University." Jenkins countered, "Who is the victor if East Carolina is denied independent university status? Who is the victor if a new door to advanced education is kept tightly closed?" The major Raleigh newspapers editorialized that Jenkins's ambitions would harm other public colleges and universities. But Raleigh television commentator Jesse Helms said in one of his nightly editorials: "In trying to destroy Leo Jenkins, his critics are actually aiming at the jugular of a great section of North Carolina which for too long and too often has been bypassed in matters of creative progress. The East Carolina College fight, then, is a fight for a region, a battle to lift the opportunities of vast numbers of North Carolinians into the happy sunlight of greater hope."

Governor Dan Moore told a joint session of the legislature: "In my judgment, if an independent university is created by this General Assembly, the structure of our system of higher education would be destroyed." After six weeks of hot debate and intense lobbying from both sides, the bill was defeated in the senate by a vote of 27 to 22.

But Governor Moore and others, concerned about a protracted battle that threatened to rip apart public higher education in the state, quickly engineered a compromise that allowed East Carolina and four others to be designated as a "regional universities," meaning they could offer master's degrees, but not doctorates. Thus, East Carolina University was born. At the same time, Western Carolina at Cullowhee, Appalachian State at Boone, North Carolina A&T at Greensboro, and North Carolina Central at Durham were also accepted into the system as regional universities. They would be administered under the Board of Higher Education and remain separate from the consolidated UNC system.

Although it wasn't the end of Colvard's ambitions for UNC Charlotte to become the precursor of a new type of urban university, his plans were certainly diminished by the fact that the legislature now had to try to accommodate the wishes, demands, and needs of more new sheep in the higher educational flock.

"The university is growing in every way," Colvard wrote in his diary. "However, we have some struggles with the legislature and the bureaucrats. To most people on the outside we seem to be moving very fast. By comparison to the rate of development of other colleges in the state we are indeed progressing. However, we need desperately to get started with some graduate programs and some new professional areas and we are ready to do so. When the present building program is completed we shall have the base for a very good small university." Later he wrote that the act creating UNC Charlotte as the fourth campus had not been matched by adequate budget increases. "In fact, there was no timetable or plan set forth for the funds that would be required to build a fourth campus that would approach the status of the three existing campuses of the consolidated university," Colvard wrote in an unpublished manuscript about the establishment of UNC Charlotte.

9 CAMPUS DISTURBANCES

Student unrest occurred all over the nation in the late 1960s as the nation dealt with the unpopular war in Vietnam and a burgeoning civil rights movement. Events reached a crescendo in the spring of 1968 with the assassination of Martin Luther King, Jr. "Black Power" became a mantra on many campuses as the youth of America seemed intent on tearing the established order apart. Some faculty members joined in with teach-ins and other attempts to be creative in reacting to the rapid changes on campus. In the 1967–68 academic year alone, the United States National Student Association reported 221 demonstrations on 101 campuses with at least 38,900 students taking part. There were 78 injuries and 417 arrests.

Dean Colvard watched news reports of the activity all over the country and worried that his campus might be next, since North Carolina institutions were not being spared. A group of black students occupied the main administration building at Duke University in Durham. At UNC Chapel Hill students boycotted the cafeteria in protest of low wages for its workers, and more student unrest was close to boiling over about the war.

"At the time these disturbances were going on I had occasion to be on the Tuskegee Institute campus in Alabama as a member of an accreditation visiting committee," Colvard recalled. "The institution had been closed for two weeks because of a disturbance involving the student occupation of an academic building and the confinement of the entire board of trustees under student surveillance for several hours. A list of demands had been presented to the administration and some rocks were thrown through windows on campus buildings, including the president's home." Colvard and the other members of the accreditation committee were warned that they might be locked in along with the trustees, although it never happened.

"We interviewed some students," he said. "I have never seen more belligerence and more scornful attitudes than we encountered among some of these black activist leaders."

UNC Charlotte was not spared some problems that appeared to be carryovers from activism of racial groups at other places in earlier years. When UNC Charlotte's predecessor institution, Charlotte College, was created in 1946, schools were still segregated. The racial problem was addressed by creating a predominantly black institution called Carver College to serve as a counterpart to Charlotte College. Carver College had been merged into the community college system before UNC Charlotte was formed.

"The fact remained that there were many black students who had not forgotten the struggles of recent years," Colvard said. "The 1954 Supreme Court decision [*Brown v. Board of Education*] and the passage of the Civil Rights Act in 1964 gave black people renewed hope for the end of racial discrimination. But the fact that black students were welcomed to the UNC Charlotte campus from the very beginning was not enough to prevent them from seeking additional rights and privileges on the new campus."

Colvard, who had proved his dedication to integration in higher education as president of Mississippi State, was sensitive to the plight of the black students at UNC Charlotte and constantly vigilant about possible demonstrations. "When King was fatally shot on April 4, 1968, a memorial service was held for him on the UNC Charlotte Campus," he said. "It was sometimes difficult to tell whether the demonstrations were based primarily on objections to the escalation of the Vietnam war and its extension into Cambodia. Memories of other tragic events such as the assassination of President John F. Kennedy in 1963 and his brother Robert in 1968 tended to encourage the organization of anti-Establishment groups."

UNC Charlotte was not a hotbed of student protest during those days, but Colvard did face a few problems. "Sometimes Charlotte students organized groups on campus and sometimes they went to other places both in and outside of North Carolina to participate in demonstrations," Colvard recalled. "A group rented the athletic department's bus, the only one we owned, to drive to Fayetteville to participate in an anti-war demonstration. A legislator who saw them use an athletic department credit card to buy gasoline called President Friday and complained although no state policy was involved."

The fact that UNC Charlotte's campus was still so undeveloped turned out to be a plus and a minus for Colvard. "The lack of maturity in organization and staffing created an environment in which communication of policies and purposes left many young and recently recruited faculty uncertain of what the future might hold for them," he said. "On the other hand, having no students residing on the campus made it somewhat more difficult for dissenting groups and riots to form."

Colvard noted that one of the prices his campus had to pay for employing a large number of bright, young, and inexperienced faculty members trained at some of the best graduate schools in the nation was that they had to mature in a new institution lacking in traditions and maturity of leadership. "Parking and dormitory regulations and the rules regarding liquor and general conduct were visibly in the process of formation at UNC Charlotte," he said. "Although we had some minor disturbances and an occasional bomb threat, we were fortunate that no bombs exploded, that we never had a riot, a building burned or even damaged, or an unmanageable confrontation among students, faculty and administrators. An occasional 'streaker' or firecracker seemed frivolous by comparison with what was happening on many campuses."

In mid-November 1968 posters appeared in the Charlotte campus's university center inviting students and faculty members to attend meetings to "bitch" about almost anything that bothered them. Black Power, student government, the administration, parking, and armed campus cops were a few of the subjects listed. An African American student urged the administration to hire black professors, increase the pay of university maids and janitors, vote black students into student government, offer a course in black history, teach African languages such as Swahili, and increase the university's black student population. A young instructor agitated one organized group by telling them they had a "Magnolia Blossom Syndrome" because they never got angry or intemperate. Aside from those distractions to studying, some faculty members became upset and complained vociferously when they were told they were going to have to begin to pay to park at university lots on campus.

At this point, one can just imagine Dean Colvard in his office on the second floor of the administration building with his head down on his desk. But his troubles were just beginning.

In December 1968, firebrand black activist Stokely Carmichael visited the campus. No substantial problems developed despite the fact that Carmichael said in his widely disseminated remarks, "All white men are my potential enemies," and "I need all the guns I can get my hands on." Colvard had to be out of town on the day Carmichael spoke, but he kept in close touch with Bonnie Cone to monitor the situation as best he could. Carmichael was accompanied by his wife, recording artist Miriam Makeba; Black Panther leader Donald Cox; and Cleveland Sellers, a leader of the Student Nonviolent Coordinating Committee. Editorials supporting Carmichael's right to visit UNCC and North Carolina A&T in Greensboro appeared in the *Greensboro Daily News,* the *Charlotte News,* and the *Gastonia Gazette.* Some members of the North Carolina legislature asked the governor, Dan Moore, to call for an investigation into the possible misuse of state funds to bring Carmichael to the campuses.

A small group of students organized themselves under the name Black Student Union. Although the administration had not recognized the group formally, it gave out press releases and sent resolutions and demands to Colvard calling for more black cheerleaders, more black faculty members, and other changes. Sometimes the requests were received in the form of threats.

Colvard recalled one example, where the Black Student Union issued a press release that ended: "We intend to confront the University and the Student Legislature Monday, February 24, 1969, at 11:30 with our demand. If our demand is not immediately met, other actions will be taken." The request was not approved and no action resulted.

The pressures of the student unrest and his attempts to propel the university's major building program along at a faster pace finally caught up with Colvard that February. He had flown to Raleigh in the North Carolina National Bank plane for a meeting with the Mecklenburg legislative delegation to discuss UNCC's budget request. On his way back to the Sir Walter Hotel, where he was staying that night, Colvard suddenly became very dizzy and incoherent. "The next thing I remember clearly was my presence in UNC Memorial Hospital in Chapel

Hill the next day," Colvard said. "They had given me a series of tests including a brain scan, a spinal puncture, electrocardiogram and others. They found nothing organically wrong but diagnosed the trouble as 'global amnesia' or 'executive's syndrome.'" He was in the hospital five days. The doctors recommended that he take some time off to rest so he and Martha left on March 3 to spend nine days in Florida trying to restore equilibrium. As a direct result of this "executive fatigue," Bill Friday again found money in his budget to give Colvard some relief from the daily grind by sending him and his wife on a study tour of fifteen so-called urban campuses in eleven states. The trips were spread out over a number of months.

"Bill was clearly looking out for me and I truly appreciated it," Colvard said.

The symbiotic relationship that Colvard and McEniry developed really paid dividends during the time following Colvard's forced vacation after his collapse in Raleigh. When Colvard returned to the campus from his hospital stay in Chapel Hill, he discovered that McEniry and Cone had been shielding him from the fact that a group of black students had presented a list of ten demands to the university administration.

The blacks gathered in front of the UNCC administration building on March 3, the same day the Colvards left for Florida, and the student leader, Ben Chavis, read the list of demands out loud to a crowd of about one hundred, including several white students who were opposing the protest. The blacks lowered the American and North Carolina flags and raised a black one on the flagpole. Tension crackled as the black and white students confronted each other. "The talk went on for about an hour," McEniry wrote in a memo that Colvard received upon his return. "We persuaded the white students not to start a fight. They reached the decision that they would not dignify this proceeding further and almost as if on signal they walked away. The black students who were left looking silly almost immediately began to break up."

The campus had also received a bomb threat on March 7, while the Colvards were still away, but no bomb was found in a search and events continued as scheduled, including a speech by Assistant Secretary of Health, Education, and Welfare (HEW) James Farmer, an African American.

Colvard returned to the campus on March 12 and began formulating his response to the ten demands made by the so-called Black Student Union. He issued it to the press on March 20 in the form of a letter to Ben Chavis. "This statement should be understood correctly as an effort to communicate with students who have concerns or have become disaffected," Colvard wrote. "It is not an answer to the 'black student union,' for no such organization has been chartered on the campus of the University of North Carolina at Charlotte."

He then listed each of the ten demands, followed by a response. The first demand was that a black studies program be initiated on campus; Colvard responded, "The University has been working toward furnishing appropriate Black Studies Programs for some time. You have already been advised that the first course has been approved and implemented."

The other demands included increasing the black student enrollment, raising the pay of university employees, implementing a pass-fail system of grading for all black students, the dismissal of all "racist" faculty members, and removing SAT requirements for entering black students. Colvard's letter concluded, "Some of the ideas that you have labeled as 'demands' are supported by the University and are in various stages of implementation, some will be given further study, and others are rejected. It is the policy of this emerging University to involve both students and faculty in the formation of policies. Any individual who feels that he does not receive just and fair treatment has the right of appeal. The University administration and I, personally, will make every effort to see that policies and procedures are just, that individual rights are respected, and that the laws laid down through democratic processes are obeyed." Despite the fact that he had been the president of Mississippi State University when it was integrated peacefully, Colvard never advertised his record in race relations and none of the students involved ever bothered to ask. Instead, his absence was called "blackitis," as if he were suffering from a disease.

The next crisis for UNC Charlotte and Colvard came on May 6, 1970, the day after four students were killed by National Guardsmen at an antiwar demonstration on the campus of Kent State in Ohio. All across the nation students were calling on others to boycott classes in protest of the Kent State shootings and the Vietnam War and to give them time off to attend antiwar rallies.

On the morning of May 6, students handed out an announcement on the UNCC campus. Titled "Student and Faculty—UNCC. You Must Be Heard," the circular said, "Encourage professors to cancel regular classes today. Postpone tests and hold classes outside at the flagpole. It is important that you don't participate in regular classes today." It also urged faculty members to support the call and said that a memorial service for the Kent State students would be held at 1 P.M. at the flag-pole in the center of the campus. "The murder of four won't silence millions," the circular ended. "Attend!!!"

Colvard attempted to defuse any potential trouble by inviting students to attend a faculty meeting. Several spoke against the war and urged the university leaders to cancel classes in support of the Kent State students. "When the process had gone on for about one hour a member of the faculty moved adjournment," Colvard recalled. "The motion, not being debatable, was seconded and unanimously passed. Other agenda items remained for another meeting. One white girl, apparently disappointed that there had been no confrontation, yelled 'pigs' as she and all others left the room." A few minutes before the 1 P.M. memorial service, Colvard learned that a student planned to hoist the Vietnam flag in place of the U.S. and North Carolina flags. Colvard was forever grateful that a student leader, Ed Wayson, stopped the student from exchanging the flags. "The memorial ceremonies proceeded with the flags at half-mast and the day came to an end without the confrontations and burning of buildings which had been so prevalent at other places," Colvard said. "Some of the oratory sounded reckless, but the crowd dispersed without any confrontation." Later that day, Colvard joined the five other chancellors of UNC campuses and President Friday in sending a telegram to North Carolina's two U.S. senators, Sam Ervin and B. Everett Jordan, urging them to support prevention of further widening of the war and to hasten its end.

The academic year finally ended and on May 20, 1970, Colvard sent a report to Friday's office saying, "Final examinations at UNCC for the 1970 spring semester are proceeding as scheduled." It had been a hectic year, prompting Colvard to write, "Needless to say, many of us were greatly relieved when examinations and commencement were concluded and students had dispersed for the summer of 1970 without experiencing the confrontations, burning and looting so prevalent on many campuses."

But not everybody was happy with Colvard's decisions and the events that had transpired on the UNCC campus. One letter Colvard received stated, "I cannot express adequately in words my extreme dismay at the way you have apparently relinquished your position as chancellor. It appears that the decisions you have allowed your faculty to make concerning protesting students (are) in complete capitulation to uninformed, unreasoning students." Another man wrote, "The action taken by your faculty as set forth in the enclosed article is stupid and void of common sense." Colvard replied to each letter he received and usually enclosed a reply such as: "As we have worked day and night during the last several weeks to seek answers to some of the grave problems which are confronting our entire nation to keep our university open and as free as possible from turmoil and destruction, we have known that it is difficult or almost impossible for the public to be fully informed of all the conditions under which we have been working. I can only assume that had you had fuller information you would not have reached the conclusion you have stated. The alterations in our schedules have been minor. We have had no deaths or destruction of property."

Despite the problems, UNCC continued to grow. "Lacking as we were in stabilized organizational structure and mature and experienced leadership, we were fortunate to have been spared disruptions with serious and damaging consequences," Colvard recalled. "It may have been because the 'establishment' was not so firmly fixed as to invite the kinds of challenges experienced by older institutions elsewhere." The first chancellor of the emerging university had been disappointed that he had been denied the five senior leaders he had requested. He was encouraged by what appeared to be a growing consensus and commitment to the fundamentals of academic excellence in the planning process.

10 COLVARD RECRUITS PAUL MILLER

It was a blustery spring day in 1968 when Dr. Dean Colvard paid a visit to his friend Dr. Paul Miller in his fourth floor office of the HEW headquarters building on Constitution Avenue in Washington, D.C. Colvard had high hopes of being able to convince Miller to give up his job as Assistant Secretary for Education of the U.S. Department of Health, Education, and Welfare to move to the fledgling campus of the University of North Carolina at Charlotte. On the surface, it would have appeared unlikely that Miller would agree to turn in his White House credentials for a job somewhere in the American hinterlands. But Colvard was as wily as the weasel who used to raid his mother's chicken house in the North Carolina mountains. Like the weasel, he had studied the situation carefully before making his move on Miller.

He knew that Miller, a Democratic appointee to the subcabinet post, probably would be out of a job in a few months, since President Lyndon B. Johnson had announced in March that he would not run again, and Colvard knew that the American public appeared to be leaning toward a new administration, one that would find a way to extract the nation from the quagmire of Vietnam. And Colvard had remembered from earlier conversations that Miller had a new wife and yearned for a new life—away from bureaucracy and paper-pushing.

Despite the fact that Miller had been hobnobbing with the denizens of the White House and had testified before Congress about the state of American education, he was ready for a change and a challenge. Although he and Colvard had not discussed the possibility of Miller's coming to Charlotte, they had talked many times about what needed to be done about higher education in the country, which was being torn apart by urban riots over civil rights and student demonstrations over the war in a far-off land. It was a time for a ray of hope somewhere somehow in the midst of burning cities and hundreds of thousands of antiwar protestors gathering on the Ellipse in Washington. The era that had seen growth in higher education explode with the return of GI Bill–financed veterans after World War II was clearly over, and a new one of uncertain focus had begun. For his part, Colvard knew Miller would bring a fresh breath of optimism about higher education to the tiny nondescript university, barely a college, in the Mid-South city of Charlotte, virtually unknown on the national scene. Many people in other parts of the country still got it mixed up with Charleston, South Carolina, and Charlottesville, Virginia.

Colvard had already recruited a competent vice chancellor for academic affairs in Hugh McEniry, and now he needed Miller badly for his experience and expertise as one of the nation's leading authorities in continuing higher education. Miller spent seventeen years at Michigan State University where he ended up as provost—second in command— before moving on to become president of his alma mater, West Virginia University. Colvard hoped that he could recruit Miller as his key man to head a strike force in planning for UNC Charlotte, and then the two of them could start to build the ideal urban university.

Miller's connections with federal funding sources also could be helpful. Colvard, who had learned how to use foundation money by watching former UNC President Frank P. Graham do the same, had already called on the Ford Foundation and others seeking funds for some of the programs at UNC Charlotte. "He had many contacts that could be useful to UNCC," Colvard recalled years later. "He was not a conventional thinker who relied on prestige and material things for his motivation."

While his taxi made its way through the Washington streets on the way to his appointment with Miller, Colvard became more excited about the possibilities: Just think, UNC Charlotte, now little more than a cow pasture with a few buildings on it, could become *the* leader in a new kind of university, higher education with a purpose, a college designed and built specifically to help shape and nurture a city.

"The idea of an urban-oriented university was well accepted by the press and an array of influential local and regional leaders of institutions and government," Colvard recalled. "It seemed to provide a timely and acceptable distinctive purpose which was complementary to and not in conflict with needs which had provided the historical purposes giving birth to other public colleges and universities in the state. We needed more than a hallmark and a goal; we needed a plan and means of implementation." He had submitted a proposal to the Reynolds and Babcock Foundations, including a salary that he considered adequate to attract a leader.

Part of the reason for approaching foundations was the fact that state appropriations of sufficient size to finance the planning process had not been forthcoming. In fact, Colvard had requested funds to hire five top leaders to assist with the planning process, but he received nothing from the legislature to accomplish this task.

Miller and Colvard came from similar backgrounds. Both grew up poor and each was the first in his family to go to college. Colvard had gone to Berea College in Kentucky, an institution that would let students work for their tuition and room and board. Miller went to West Virginia University, and his father had mortgaged the farm to pay the tuition and room and board. Colvard had gotten his master's degree at the University of Missouri and then gone on for his doctorate at Purdue. Miller received his both his master's and doctorate in 1953 in sociology and anthropology at Michigan State. Colvard had become a dean of agriculture at North Carolina State University and then president of Mississippi State University in 1960. He had proved his mettle in Mississippi as president of Mississippi State. The smooth, soft-voiced Miller, of average height and slight build, had been president of West Virginia University in 1962–68, where he had served until HEW Secretary John Gardner had recruited him to join him in Washington on August 1, 1966.

At the time of their rendezvous in Washington in the spring of 1968, Colvard was fifty-five, old enough to have learned that the opportunity to do something truly creative comes rarely, if ever, in one's professional life, especially if that professional life was in higher education administration. Miller was forty-nine and of the same mindset and opinion. In other words, they both had served as chiefs of large public universities, but both yearned for a major breakthrough in how those institutions were operated and how they adjusted to serve an urbanizing society.

As his taxi bumped along from his hotel to Miller's office, Colvard recalled the hours he and Miller had spent discussing the need for change. They had met as members of various committees of the National Association of State Universities and Land-Grant Colleges. Each had served as president of the association's Council of Presidents. Both Miller and Colvard had become very concerned that the era of the rural and farming emphasis was changing and that the nation needed a new phase of education, one they called "urban-oriented" colleges and universities. The idea was to send urban extension agents out to work with urban dwellers. It was a concept that had never been tried.

"I needed Paul very badly," Colvard recalled. "He understood the concept of the urban university, and I was having to devise ways and means of maintaining some senior leadership ability on my staff and to have people who would automatically be respected, academically, by the young professors we were hiring." McEniry and Miller were the first two experienced leaders he wanted on board to provide role models and leaders in cooperation with the Charlotte College faculty he had inherited and young faculty members being recruited.

Colvard also needed Miller because he, Colvard, knew he would be tied up in interminable meetings—with faculty members, with community leaders, with political leaders and others—but Miller would be free to think and act creatively to put together the best plan possible, unfettered by the regular trappings of academic administrative duties.

Once he had reached Miller's office and they sat facing each other, Colvard started his spiel to attract his friend to come to work and live in Charlotte. Colvard knew that Miller's first wife had died suddenly in 1964 and that Miller had remarried in January 1966. He and his new wife, Francena, had lived in Morgantown for only a few months before moving to Washington, where she took a job as national executive director of the American Association of University Women. As they settled in for their discussion, Colvard said, "Paul, we've been arguing about what adult education is and I think we've pretty well agreed that it is education for use. We've been arguing about where it should fit into a university's structure of things and we aren't certain about where the leader should report. Why don't you come down to Charlotte and help me mobilize the knowledge to plan a university? In planning it we'll let circumstances develop that determine where it ends up in the administrative structure. What I need for you to do is apply those principles to planning a university."

For his part, while responding to invitations from Cornell and Syracuse to consider professorships as well as the presidency of the Rochester Institute of Technology, Miller remembered thinking, "We both knew we didn't want to stay in Washington and that our family and professional values lay in a return to teaching and scholarship. While our interest in Syracuse had grown, Dean's offer looked like a good opportunity. We liked Dean and Martha [Colvard's wife] and trusted them." Colvard's offer was not as much a surprise as an outsider might have imagined. In actuality, Miller had been thinking about the development of an urban university for years, and in the back of his mind he hoped that somehow he could be a part of one. "It had to be a laboratory, if it was going to be a leader among universities," he recalled. "I had in mind of having these kind of places spring up. The shift from rural to urban emphasis was coming."

As part of his new job with HEW, Miller had chaired a joint legislative committee charged with finding solutions to the whole urban crisis that had been brought on by the Vietnam War protests and civil rights uprising, which was made worse by the assassination of Martin Luther King, Jr., in May 1968.

The fact that Charlotte presented a clean slate also was very important to Miller. All the other possible universities where he might be able to try innovation already were encumbered with set plans. In Charlotte, the opportunity to be *the* planner, to set the agenda, and to put theories into practice for once was very attractive, despite the fact that the university was only three years old and had less than three thousand students. In his installation address on March 3, 1967, Colvard had said, "We do not have a detailed blueprint setting forth all of our future development. Our hope is that we may operate more as an organism than as a robot." Miller had been doing more than thinking about a new urban university concept. "I had been trying to get the White House interested in continuing education," he recalled. And he and others in the Johnson administration had even gone so far as to propose legislation, which was adopted but never funded, caught up in the backlash against Johnson's pro-war stance. "In Charlotte, I wanted to study this thing, consult on it, write about it and here's a place where I can do it," Miller said. Colvard pumped him up even further. Miller recalled, "He told me it would be a learning society. We would be learning from each other—professors from students, students from professors, townspeople from professors, professors from townspeople, board from faculty, trustees from students, students from trustees. All these things would be involved. We would have a learning community, a learning society in the nature of the university and there we would simply open up the university and we would welcome in the community."

The concept of the urban university was not that new in 1968, although no pure model had been developed. Miller and Colvard had both read University of Wisconsin at Milwaukee Chancellor J. Martin Klotsche's book, *The Urban University and the Future of Our Cities,* which had been published in 1966, the year Colvard was named the first chancellor of UNC Charlotte. Charlotte was not even mentioned in Klotsche's book, which purported to be an overview of the status and future of urban or metropolitan universities. But Miller and Colvard could see that the principles Klotsche listed about the needs and goals of an urban university could be applied to the Charlotte campus in North Carolina's largest city. The urban university's central task, he wrote, should be "to understand the city, to analyze its problems, to research and comment about them, to commit university resources and to enlist those of the community so that the quality of urban life can be improved. For the insights of the humanist and philosopher, the social scientist, the scientist and engineer, and the artist can all be employed to help our cities fulfill the promise of urban living." Miller and Colvard took those words to heart and believed they could see a way to put them into practice at Charlotte, which provided a clean slate and an ideal laboratory.

Miller's boss in Washington, John Gardner, had been widely recognized as one of the country's leading authorities in education. As chief executive officer of the Carnegie Corporation in New York City, Gardner had written in 1957 about the need for urban universities to fulfill a role that others, such as small liberal arts colleges, could not. University of California president Clark Kerr had voiced similar notions.

Klotsche emphasized that the urban university had a unique mission. "It is in a position to do things that other institutions cannot," he wrote. "The university comes closest to being able to identify itself with the whole of the urban scene and a total concern for the city. . . . Universities can provide a fresh point of view and devise new techniques of dealing with the increasingly complex problems of our metropolitan areas. The university should clearly be the leader and at the same time reflect the spirit of the times." Klotsche recommended setting up an Urban Observatory in each city as a counterpart to the old agricultural field stations under the land-grant system. These new observatories would be staffed by university professors and students to study city problems and experiment with solutions, and if some were found, transmit them to city leaders and other cities.

Miller knew that there was support in Washington for programs that could be produced by urban universities, such as the new one being developed in Charlotte. He knew because his ultimate boss in Washington, President Johnson, had broached the subject in a June 20, 1964, speech at the opening of the new campus of the University of California at Irvine. Johnson said that such a new university could improve the plight of the cities "just as our colleges and universities changed the future of our farms a century ago." The president then asked, "Why not an urban extension service, operated by universities across the country and similar to the Agricultural Extension Service that assists rural areas?"

This was a concept that Miller and Colvard were familiar with, since both had led major land-grant universities, Miller at West Virginia University and Colvard at NC State and Mississippi State. The land-grant institutions had been created in 1862 to use Agricultural Extension agents to take the results of research into new and better ways to grow crops and animals out into the field. Eventually, Ag Extension agents were located in every state in the nation. The Agricultural Extension Service "has contributed substantially in achieving the dramatic shift from food shortages to substantial surpluses, and in raising the standard of living enjoyed by farm people to among the highest in the world," Klotsche noted.

The idea of transferring the concept to urban extension agents had been around as early as 1948, when it was mentioned in a white paper in a study commission at the U.S. Department of Agriculture. Paul Ylvisaker of the Ford Foundation had mentioned in it a 1958 report. "Urbanites, no less than their rural predecessors, need help with family budgets, nutrition, maintenance, land use, housing, vocational guidance, credit, and conservation," Ylvisaker wrote. "And these urban extension services, no less than those provided by agricultural agents, need to be backed with continuous research of the scale and sophistication long ago developed through the agricultural experiment stations." In his book, Klotsche called for a new kind of "urban agent" who would move into the inner core of cities and "give the university a physical presence it does not now have. But the entire university must become involved. A team approach, using the skills of a number of disciplines, holds much more promise than the use of a single agent with only generalized knowledge."

Johnson did not stop with the speech in Irvine. On January 12, 1965, in his message on education to Congress, he urged universities to step up their research to find solutions to urban problems. "Faculty must be called upon for consulting activities," he said. "Pilot projects, seminars, conferences, TV programs, and task forces drawing on many departments of the university—all should be brought into play." Johnson signed Title I of the Higher Education Act of 1965 on November 8, 1965, to make it possible for universities to develop continuing higher education projects with emphasis on urban issues. And it was part of Miller's job in Washington to see that such programs were instituted.

"The idea was to recast Title I to support some fifty cities in the nation with an urban university," Miller said. "Not to create them anew, but to take Wayne State or Temple or Wright University in Dayton and to make what we were trying to create from scratch in Charlotte."

But the program failed to gain adequate funding from the Congress, which was mired down in antiwar rhetoric following the riots of 1968. So Miller decided that he would go to Charlotte to try to see if the urban university concept could be created there through state-funding sources and used as a model for other states. His title would be director of university planning studies and distinguished professor of education. In reality, he would be in charge of planning the university and acting as a mentor for young faculty members. "One of the reasons I answered this call was that I decided if we could do something really unique and creative in Charlotte, since we had an open playing field, maybe then we could get the Temples and the Wayne States and the others, and we could have in each city an urban university as we have in each state a land-grant university."

Charlotte, by virtue of its suburban location, could avoid another problem that Klotsche pointed out. "All urban universities, public or private, large or small, single or multi-purpose, in blighted areas or in attractive residential sections, are struggling with their environment," he wrote. "Burgeoning enrollments, limited acreage, high land costs, problems of renewal and conservation, face every urban campus."

After their meeting in March of 1968, Miller told Colvard he was very interested and would talk it over with his wife. Colvard hoped it wasn't a bad omen that he discovered he had left his wallet in Miller's office and was unable to pay the taxi driver. "We had to drive back over to Paul's office to get it," he recalled.

Within a few days, Miller called Colvard and told him he and his wife had agreed to go to Charlotte to try to help build a dream. "I knew that within the state university system there would be a lot of jealousy among the other institutions," Miller said. "But I was hoping they we could avoid becoming just like everyone else, bottom-line oriented, really becoming vocational."

Colvard agreed to help find a job in Charlotte for Miller's wife (she became a professor at Queens College) and the deal was sealed. As he awaited Miller's arrival that September, Colvard was pleased to preside over the May 26, 1968, graduation ceremonies, when UNC Charlotte awarded its first honorary degrees to Frank Porter Graham and Addison Reese. Charlotte would be the Millers' new home as of September 1, 1968, and Paul Miller and Dean Colvard would now have a chance to make their dream of a new type of university come true.

With Miller's commitment Colvard advised the Reynolds and Babcock Foundations that he could fulfill the first part of his plan for planning—he had found a planning leader. Both James Hilton of the Smith Reynolds Foundation and William Archie of the Babcock Foundation were pleased with the news. They knew Miller and could not have been more satisfied.

11

MILLER GOES
TO WORK

Paul Miller had gone about his new work enthusiastically. His wife had begun teaching at Queens College in Charlotte, and their teenage son, Thomas, seemed to like his new school. Miller was hard at work reading, researching, and writing plans for an unheard-of type of university. "The UNCC plan held promise as an institution that might properly become the prototype of an 'urban-grant' institution," he wrote in his unpublished autobiography. "It could build from the experience of the 'land-grant' university while free of the obligation to reconcile traditional obligations to rural society. To be sure, the basic requisites of any university had to be developed. But, for me, a new kind of university for a new kind of society was the cutting edge of my assignment in Charlotte."

Miller, with Colvard's assent, began bringing a succession of experts in different disciplines to the UNCC campus to help shape the plan. "By March of 1969, UNCC planning was well on its way," Miller wrote in his memoir. "Both philosophy and methodology for the planning effort were proving adequate." In addition to his planning duties, Miller was traveling to Raleigh once a week to teach a graduate seminar in adult education at NC State, and he was shoehorning in time to work on a book on university outreach that he had promised for the W. K. Kellogg Foundation.

While Miller was finding his new job satisfying and challenging, another even more exciting opportunity to experiment with the urban university concept arose, one that eventually he felt he could not turn down because of his unique background connected with it. As U.S. Assistant Secretary for Education at HEW, Miller had helped put together a plan to move the nation's second largest college for the deaf, the National Institute for the Deaf, into a merger with the Rochester Institute of Technology in New York. In April of 1969, when Miller had been at UNCC only eight months, an executive head-hunting firm called to ask him to recommend prospects for the presidency of RIT, where the man who had been president for thirty-two years was finally retiring. Miller recommended five men, but at the end of the conversation the headhunter asked if he could include Miller on the list. Miller hesitated and then said he would talk it over with his wife and call him back. After a night of discussion, he and Francena decided to at least take a look before making a decision. A whirlwind of activity followed, with the Millers visiting Rochester and eventually deciding that the opportunity was just too exciting and interesting to turn down.

Thirty years later, Miller would note in his autobiography: "Rochester Institute of Technology, since 1829 with deep roots in Greater Rochester's past, was itself facing, not unlike UNCC, a new future as an urban university: the institution had just moved its eight colleges to a splendid new campus, to which the NTID campus would be added later. My first and only trip to Rochester and RIT had been in 1968 to collaborate on selecting the site for NTID." With a note of regret for having to leave Colvard and Charlotte and having to abandon a career in teaching and studying again, Miller saw the Rochester post as a once-in-a-lifetime chance to pursue the idea of a private urban university as opposed to a public one. He wrote in his memoir: "Most challenging was Rochester as an urban metropolitan region: an older city of medium size, possessed of strong educational and cultural resources, being challenged by urban tensions and change, and surely by transformations in industry and profession then appearing on the horizon. Not unlike Charlotte, it was a place to advance the ideas of an unusual urban university."

Colvard accepted Miller's news with a tinge of regret and sadness, but he understood Miller's reasons and knew he and Miller had no choice but to move on with their lives and careers.

Miller let the public know in a speech to the Charlotte Rotary Club on September 16, 1969, just fifteen days before he was due to report to

RIT. In the speech he paid tribute to Colvard as a man of vision and leadership and warned that the goal of developing UNCC into a leading urban university would be difficult to achieve. "Chancellor Colvard is in process of bringing about a new kind of academic administration," Miller said. "He is, as we both might say in our traditional vernacular, 'ploughing new ground.' As a humane person, he is allowing his humaneness to flow into the sinews of the institution. He has followed with invitations to all to fully participate in the central feature of planning the institution's future. With a quiet and sympathetic magic, he has helped find tasks of importance and, then, guide people into teams qualified to tackle them. And he has not blinked when ideas outlandishly breaking all precedent come suddenly upon the table." Despite the high quality of Colvard's leadership, Miller cautioned the Rotarians, which at that time included many of Charlotte's top business executives, that "the odds are against" being able to create anything other than a conventional university in Charlotte. "The give and take of competition in state-supported systems nips at and endangers boldness," he said.

As an outsider with considerable experience in higher education, Miller was uniquely qualified to comment on UNCC's status. "UNCC is superbly on its way," he continued in the Rotary Club speech. "From the uniqueness of its history to the imagination of its planning, its future seems assured as a large and competent center of education and culture. A small army of people have made it possible, following the lead of such stellar leaders as Cone and Colvard. But now it faces the consequences, the follow-through, on its intentions. If it is successful, UNCC will emerge as the forerunner of a new kind of university in a new America. Its presence may do something else as well, given the vision, will and self-confidence, to lead amid a great number of metropolitan institutions and agencies in helping greater Charlotte become a 'learning community,' a university itself in outlook and behavior. Then would we find programs designed for all ages, the absence of specific rituals, no predetermined requirements for learning, and a genuine schedule and encouragement for continuous lifelong learning. Campus residence halls of special design would be devoted to retirees, from which they could both learn and reach out to the community as volunteers to enrich the civic culture. These imaginations now reside in the UNCC plan. But alas, we must face its consequences, and, despite the traditional obstacles and those which may rise anew, proceed with implementation. My best wishes and my support, if and whenever needed, go with you."

Miller's warning did not fall on deaf ears, but political pressures that had built up over the years for recognition of public institutions of higher education throughout the state would result in even more regional universities in the immediate future and consequently threaten the golden dream that Miller and Colvard had for using UNC Charlotte as the model of the new urban university, not just for North Carolina, but for the nation as well.

Colvard's disappointment when Miller resigned was relieved considerably by the great progress that had resulted from Miller's effective leadership in executing the first phase of the planning program. With the assistance of Miller's associate, Dorothea Lakin, and Colvard's assistant, Ben Romine, the plan for planning was pursued to its completion and reported in a booklet, "Emergence of a University."

Although Miller's tenure was short, Colvard considered his planning studies an important example of what he had been calling the "organic process" in planning a university. Miller had invited more than sixty respected senior academic leaders from many of the nation's leading graduate universities to seminars at UNCC with the young faculty and the recently appointed department heads and deans in seventeen disciplines. These interactions served as the basis for brilliant young academicians to participate in planning their own new university. Colvard believed that their feelings of ownership would strengthen their commitment to build a university of excellence. He also believed that their early involvement would tend to create long-range stability when faced with changing administrative structures.

Colvard moved to solidify the gains Miller had wrought in planning by asking his administrative assistant, Ben Romine, to assume the planning leadership as director of planning and institutional studies. Colvard considered himself fortunate to have had outstanding administrative assistants to take on the important building roles. His first, Julian Mason, helped him compose his installation address. His second, Doug Orr, became a vice chancellor and later president of Warren Wilson College. Romine was his third. Earl Backman succeeded him and became the first director of the International Studies Program. Bill Steimer, an attorney, became Colvard's final administrative assistant and also served as the UNCC legal counsel. Orr succeeded Bonnie Cone as vice chancellor for student affairs and, Cone's assistant, Dennis Rash, became dean of students. While McEniry had been in Cullowhee, Dr. Phil Hildreth had become acting vice chancellor for academic affairs, and Louis W. Moelchert, Jr., had been recruited as vice chancellor for business affairs. Their individual and composite capabilities and their commitment to building a first-class, urban-oriented university were a source of continuing strength to Colvard.

12 A CHANGE
      OF COURSE

As Dean Colvard returned to Charlotte after his successful trip to recruit Paul Miller, he was feeling terrific. After all, he was the chancellor of the first new university to be created in North Carolina in seventy-four years. He had convinced Miller to come on board, and he had solidified the support of Charlotte leaders, the governor, the legislature, and the president of the consolidated university system, Bill Friday. In essence, he felt he had been given a blank page to sketch the plan for a new type of university, one that would render invaluable assistance not only to the Charlotte urban region, but perhaps to urban regions all over the nation.

"The spirit of UNCC is improving," Colvard wrote in his diary at the time. "Almost everyone seems to share in a positive outlook for the future. With the coming of Dr. Miller came grants from Smith Reynolds and Babcock Foundations to get our academic planning program formalized and under way." The executive directors of the Reynolds and Babcock foundations, both former top educational executives, were supporters of the plan for planning and of the recruitment of Miller as the leader.

But things are not always as they seem, and Colvard's rosy optimism soon took a drastic hit as the shape of higher education in North Carolina was twisted into a new configuration. Lieutenant Governor Robert W. Scott had watched all the legislative activity as UNC Charlotte was becoming part of the state university system. He had stayed in the background as Governor Dan K. Moore had to wrestle with the aims and ambitions of politicians and higher educators from East Carolina and the other various public colleges from all regions of the state. But as the election of 1968 approached, signaling the end of Moore's four-year term, Scott, who had been elected lieutenant governor in 1964, suddenly became a major figure in the battle over the future of state-supported higher education.

The son of W. Kerr Scott, who had been a popular state commissioner of agriculture, governor, and U.S. senator, Bob Scott had not been expected to enter politics. He said his father had often told him that one politician in the family was enough, and since his graduation from NC State in 1952 Bob had spent most of his time watching over the family's 1,800-acre dairy farm near Haw River. His father, who had had been elected governor in 1948 and became a U.S. senator in 1954, died in 1958, and young Bob was content to stay on the farm until September 1963. At an annual dove hunt at his uncle state senator Ralph Scott's adjacent farm, several old-time Scott supporters urged him to test the waters for a run at governor. He made a few calls across the state only to find he had started too late to raise enough money, and some party leaders thought he was too young—at thirty-five—and too inexperienced, having never held public office.

He considered running for Congress, commissioner of agriculture, or lieutenant governor, finally deciding on the lieutenant governorship because his mentor, Ben Roney, a wily, longtime political power-behind-the-scenes from Rocky Mount, suggested that the second-ranking post might be a good way for Scott to gain experience and exposure for a gubernatorial run four years away. Scott took his advice and went up against former state house speaker Clifton Blue and state senator John Jordan. Although Scott led in the first primary, he failed to get enough votes to win outright, and Blue called for a runoff. He beat Blue in the second primary after Jordan threw his support to him.

So when 1968 rolled around, Scott was positioned to seek the Democratic nomination as governor. But no son of a governor had ever been elected to the high post, and no lieutenant governor had ever won direct election as governor. In addition, Scott faced formidable opposition in the person of J. Melville Broughton, Jr., of Raleigh, himself the son of a governor. Also in the Democratic primary was an African American dentist from Charlotte, Dr. Reginald Hawkins, the first of his race to run for governor. The winner would face stiff Republican opposition in the November general election from restaurant chain owner James C. Gardner of Rocky Mount.

After a flurry of campaigning throughout the state, Scott won the Democratic primary handily over Broughton, with Hawkins finishing a distant third. Then in November, Scott won again, this time by 84,000 votes of more than 1.5 million cast. When he was inaugurated in January 1969 at the age of thirty-nine, he became the youngest North Carolina governor in the twentieth century. Although he was much younger than most of the state's other political leaders, Bob Scott quickly proved that he was cut from the same maverick cloth as his famous father.

The young governor was soon confronted with major problems, none of his own making. The unpopular war in Vietnam had spawned student demonstrations on nearly every campus in the United States, and North Carolina was to be no exception. Civil rights demonstrations also continued in every major city.

Scott, who portrayed himself as a populist in the manner of his father, had attended Duke University for two years in pre-med before his grades in science-related courses convinced him that his future lay elsewhere. That was when he transferred to North Carolina State University, where he majored in dairy husbandry and where he encountered a supportive animal science department head named Dr. Dean Colvard, who had joined the university in 1947 and become a department head in 1948. For the rest of his life, Scott would credit Colvard as his mentor.

In fact, Scott had a student job in the university-owned dairy barn, and Colvard was in charge of the payroll. "My dad and mom paid my basic expenses, but if I wanted anything else I had to work for it," Scott said. He spent a lot of time in Colvard's office, because Colvard, as the department head, handed out the paychecks and had an attractive secretary who always had a box of chocolates on hand for visitors. "He always seemed to have time for the students," Scott recalled. "He and my dad were pretty close," he said. "Therefore, the name Dean Colvard was in my mind pretty often." When he became governor, Bob Scott named Colvard to the state awards commission and appointed him vice chairman of a new group, the North Carolina Council on Policies and Goals, a sort of think tank created to consider what the state ought to be doing to prepare for the future.

Colvard had first met Kerr Scott in 1938 when Scott was the state commissioner of agriculture interviewing candidates who wanted to become director of the North Carolina State Agricultural Experiment Station at Swannanoa, just east of Asheville. Colvard had heard that the director would be expected to raise money from the station's staff members to support the state Democratic party, and he volunteered to Scott that he would not have anything to do with that approach. Scott told him, "Now, Colvard, you just do a good job for me and that's the only type of politics you will be expected to play." Their paths would cross many more times in the next twenty years, and they corresponded right up until Scott's death in 1958, when Colvard was dean of the School of Agriculture at NC State in Raleigh. He had received a letter of congratulations from Kerr Scott when he became dean in 1953.

Bob Scott, who described himself as a "let-the-chips-fall" kind of guy, did not shrink from problems when he became governor. He set about reorganizing state government from 300 to 25 administrative levels, and he warned that he was determined to restructure public higher education. "I had some rough edges, no question about it," Scott recalled years later.

But when he became governor, he knew that he had to do something about the political infighting and intense lobbying that supporters of the public colleges and universities were carrying on in Raleigh. He and Colvard, who had been chancellor at UNCC since 1966, discussed the situation. Scott recalled, "We had several conversations about the need to 'do something' to improve the administrative structure of the university system, to at least lessen, if not eliminate, the fierce competition of the various . . . institutions . . . fighting for money in the legislature and also a better way of controlling what programs would be approved at what institutions rather than the individual institutions going directly to the legislature. The classic example at that time of course was Dr. Leo Jenkins when he was fighting so hard for the medical school."

Scott said he and NC State chancellor John Caldwell also had discussed the need for a consolidation of all the state-supported senior colleges and universities.

Caldwell's and Colvard's discussions with Scott had to be confidential, since Caldwell and Colvard answered to the consolidated university's board of trustees, and the board's executive committee was opposed to Scott's proposal to bring all state-supported senior colleges and universities under one governing board. "They could express their views, but they couldn't go to the legislature and fight for it because nobody knew who was going to win that fight and if they came out on the short end of it they might be in big trouble," Scott said.

For many years the governor had served as chairman of the board of trustees for the university. Recent legislation had also made the governor chairman of the Board of Higher Education. This brought him directly into the conflict between these two top boards. He appointed a committee known as the Warren Commission to make a study and advise him. The debate had become extended and acrimonious and ultimately led to the creation of a board of governors to oversee the entire system of public higher education in North Carolina, a solution that Colvard regarded as sound.

Miller's planning studies involving many of the young faculty members at UNCC with leading scholars in their fields from major universities gave confidence that planning was sound, regardless of the overall administrative structure. Although Colvard had favored some kind of overall governing board, which Friday opposed, Colvard also felt that Friday was the person who should lead such a board. Although Paul Miller resigned to head a large private university before final plans were drawn, Colvard was confident that the planning program at UNCC had advanced far enough to be deeply implanted in the minds of the faculty. In his faculty convocation address, he said, "There is nothing decisive that can be said at this time concerning the possible outcome of the debate bearing on the subject of restructuring higher education in our state. . . . The only thing that seems certain is that this issue will continue to create lively debate until it is settled. While the outcome is unpredictable, I believe very strongly that if we can be constructive and creative in our efforts to respond to high-priority educational needs, our institution will thrive regardless of the administrative structure which may emerge. It is not the administrative structure that makes a university. It is the quality of work in the classroom and the quality of interaction between students and faculty that make a university great or mediocre. It is in this area that we have expertise." Colvard's idea of involving Miller in pairing young faculty members with visiting mentors led to strong and effective planning participation by a very young faculty that made UNCC unique and led to long-lasting and loyal faculty leaders.

While the debate over the future of North Carolina's higher educational institutions continued to rage, Scott said he talked with others, including UNC president Bill Friday and Cameron West, executive director of the state Board of Higher Education, who both agreed that something had to be done, but Scott also looked outside the state for ideas. "Georgia was my model," he recalled. "They had a small university board of regents. There were a few other states that had something like that, but they had already started. They didn't have to go to the battlefield that we did to get it done. As a result of that I was able to play a leading role in the Educational Commission of the States and to some extent the Southern Regional Education Board."

Although Scott, in his inauguration speech, had called for the inclusion of the colleges at Asheville and Wilmington into the consolidated university, he recalled that he had no plan at that time to bring others under one umbrella. "I really didn't have a feel for how 'bad' or what a mess this higher education thing was until I had been in office for a while," Scott recalled. The legislature authorized the Asheville and Wilmington campuses being brought into the UNC system in April 1969, and Scott became even more determined to bring order to the chaos by bringing all the UNC campuses and the so-called regional universities and other public colleges under the control of a single governing board.

Scott described the situation as this: the leaders of the executive committee of the consolidated university, which consisted of campuses at Chapel Hill, Raleigh, Greensboro, Charlotte, Asheville, and Wilmington, did not want other campuses taken in because they felt it would dilute the university's influence and power, especially regarding funding from the legislature. The other state-supported institutions were having to lobby the legislature for "crumbs off the table," Scott said. The state Board of Higher Education, which was supposed to have control over all public colleges and universities, actually had very little power, since the consolidated university and the nonaffiliated colleges simply made end runs around the board to the legislature.

UNC president Bill Friday fought Scott's reorganization plan furiously, but mostly behind closed doors. "In a statement denouncing the restructuring plan, he (Friday) warned that it would deconsolidate the university system and 'effectively dismantle the unified and highly successful' efforts of the six-campus system," according to Link's biography of Friday. Scott said Leo Jenkins definitely brought lobbying the legislature to a new level. "But all of them had been going to the legislature," he said. "That was the way they had to do it. They went directly to the legislature to get what they could. The greater university, that is Chapel Hill, NC State, UNC Greensboro, their trustees, they had the power and the influence. They would always dominate. . . . and as you might expect the so-called poor institutions, predominantly black institutions, and Pembroke, they got the least amount of crumbs. It was inherently unfair." But Scott said the situation slowly began to change as graduates of institutions such as East Carolina, Appalachian State, and Western Carolina became more numerous and more powerful in the legislature.

"The influence and the power of the UNC graduates became diluted," he said. "These other institutions began to go to their legislators and the competition became much more fierce. It was logrolling and a good example of course was when almost overnight they were designated universities. All of a sudden everybody was a university and we became somewhat the laughing stock of the country."

The governor brought the situation to a head with a speech on May 25, 1971, to the combined houses of the General Assembly. "For some time we have been traveling a dangerously erratic course in public higher education," he said. "We are proceeding with all sail and no rudder. Wasteful and damaging forces are chipping away at the structure of our system. Disaster will follow unless it is righted, reinforced, and redirected. We needed to do this long ago. We must do it now. Tomorrow will be too late. Most of the damage is occurring from within—the wrangling, the rivalry, the empire building, the costly overlapping and duplication, the gilding-of-the-lily, the arrogant distrust and suspicion, the holier-than-thou, looking-down-the-nose attitude, the devil-take-the-hindmost."

In an interview decades later, Scott said he never worried about a possible loss of influence on UNCC's part. "It was going to grow anyway," he said. "It didn't have any problems. It was going to grow by its location. And I think that was the reason Bill Friday and the university board of trustees were so willing to bring Charlotte into the university system to begin with because they knew."

Despite stiff resistance, Scott's view finally prevailed. In a special session in October 1971, the legislature approved a bill consolidating all public colleges and universities under one governing board. "My view is that the act which passed is much better than I was afraid it might be," Colvard noted in his diary at the time. "The new structure will be effective only if proper leadership can be mobilized. It is assumed that Bill Friday will become President of the system. He is by far the best qualified person." Friday was indeed selected as president and held the post until his retirement in 1986, when he was replaced by a Charlottean, C. D. "Dick" Spangler, Jr.

Through all the discussions and machinations about restructuring higher education, Colvard remained optimistic, and when it was all over he pronounced himself satisfied that the right thing had been done. "We have a very good structure for all of higher education," he wrote in his diary in November 1971. "Our problem now is to develop attitudes and to select and organize leaders to make it work." He issued a statement to the public that endorsed the proposal. "Being a part of the Consolidated University has benefited UNCC in many ways," he said. "The great prestige of the University of North Carolina in national education circles has made faculty recruitment much easier. A new institution, virtually unknown in educational circles, would have had more difficulties and less success without this association."

As the year drew to a close, Colvard took stock of his five years at the helm. "I have now been at UNCC almost as long as I was at Mississippi State University," he wrote in his diary. "I am very proud that at both places many new programs have been set in motion. UNCC is now larger in enrollment than MSU was when I went there. In another five years we will catch up with them in enrollment. But fifty years will be required to have retired alumni returning in large numbers. I still think it is fun to build a new university, but I readily admit that there are moments of loneliness. Some of the national connections and prestige had to be sacrificed for the rewards of knowing that something new is being created. While I am still glad I came to Charlotte, I would advise others to make such a move only after fully evaluating the pros and cons. Had I not anticipated some of the negatives I would have been discouraged. However, the development has been every bit as fast as I could have anticipated."

13

THE COLLEGE OF
ARCHITECTURE IS BORN

Although it flourished under Chancellor Colvard's leadership, UNC Charlotte's College of Architecture was an idea whose time had come a few months even before there was a UNC Charlotte. The idea to develop a second architecture school to complement the program at the School of Design at NC State in Raleigh originated with Leslie Boney, Jr., of Wilmington, who was president of the North Carolina Chapter of the American Institute of Architects in 1965. Boney appointed a study committee headed by Charlotte architect S. Scott Ferebee, Jr., and including Robert L. Clemmer of Raleigh and B. Atwood Skinner, Jr., of Wilson.

As chairman of the committee, Ferebee wrote to President Bill Friday and UNCC's acting chancellor Bonnie Cone on October 1, 1965, proposing the idea of creating the architecture school at Charlotte since the new campus had been approved in July 1965. In his letter, Ferebee noted that Dean Henry Kamphoefner of the School of Design at NC State and NC State Chancellor John T. Caldwell supported the idea of another school of architecture. At a meeting of the North Carolina Design Foundation on December 1, 1965, Dean Kamphoefner indicated that the School of Design was approaching a maximum enrollment of 450 students. He recommended the establishment of another architecture school at another campus of the University of North Carolina. Caldwell agreed but urged that the matter not be discussed publicly until it could be explored further in academic circles. Friday talked to Ferebee and Boney by telephone and suggested that the matter await the selection of the first chancellor at the Charlotte campus.

"I became the first chancellor on April 1, 1966, and Mr. Ferebee wrote to me on May 10, 1966, suggesting a need for about thirty-five more graduate architects than the state was producing at that time," Colvard recalled. "Apparently, the number graduating in architecture from the NC State School of Design was about that same number and Mr. Ferebee's indication was that it needed to be doubled. In all of his communications Ferebee emphasized the importance of urban planning."

Colvard acted quickly on the architects' suggestion and gave it a high priority. On August 11, 1966, in his first personnel move at Charlotte, he named Larry G. Owen as director of institutional research and told him his first assignment was to assemble the information needed to support a sound decision concerning the establishment of a new school of architecture at the new campus. Owen immediately wrote to Richard R. Whitaker, Jr., director of educational programs at the American Institute of Architects (AIA), seeking a meeting for information that might contribute to assembling the new data.

Colvard suggested that the architects expand their committee to take in members from other parts of the state. Consequently Macon Smith, who had succeeded Boney as North Carolina chairman, added Anthony Lord of Asheville and William Freeman, Jr., of High Point to the group.

The committee took its report to the full North Carolina membership at the annual state convention in July, recommending adoption of a resolution calling for a new school at Charlotte and pointing out that there was a need for another school since there was an acute statewide shortage of trained architects. The resolution, adopted by the full convention, said that "when its present expansion is complete, the School of Design at North Carolina State University will have reached optimum size and further expansion will not be in the best interest of the school or its students and with this capacity it will not be able to meet the immediate year to year needs for architectural graduates in North Carolina." The proposal was submitted to the UNC board and appropriate legislative committees, but failed to win approval for inclusion in the 1967 budget. It resurfaced in 1968 and 1969 and finally won legislative approval with an $89,117 appropriation to begin in 1970 with a small core staff. It was estimated that the initial enrollment in 1971–72 would be 100 students, increasing successively to 175, 275, 375, and 450. An architecture building would cost $2.2 million in 1973–74.

On September 2, 1969, Ferebee wrote to state senator Herman A. Moore of the Mecklenburg County legislative delegation: "On behalf of the architects of North Carolina and the South Atlantic region, I wish to thank you for your efforts in obtaining approval from the General Assembly for the establishment of a new School of Architecture at the University of North Carolina at Charlotte. In talking with other legislators, with other architects in the Raleigh area, and with Chancellor Colvard, all are of the opinion that your leadership and determined efforts were primarily responsible for the funds being included in the budget for this much needed facility."

In January of 1970 Colvard assembled a high-profile ad hoc group of academic experts in architecture training to come to Charlotte for a two-day planning conference. Included were deans of relatively new architecture schools—Lawrence W. Anderson of the Massachusetts Institute of Technology, Charles P. Graves of the University of Kentucky, John W. Hill of the University of Maryland, and B. N. Lacy of the University of Tennessee. They spent a weekend helping Colvard and his staff draw up guidelines for the new school. Colvard said later that, since they had no architecture faculty, this experience involving himself and McEniry helped him to form the "plan for planning" submitted to the Reynolds and Babcock Foundations.

The chancellor and McEniry then began interviewing candidates to head the program. Architecture Dean Bruno Leon of the University of Detroit and Director of Graduate Studies O. Jack Mitchell of Rice University came to Charlotte for interviews. After more recruiting, Robert G. Anderson of the architecture program at the University of Miami was hired as chairman of the new division of architecture at UNCC. "I had met Robert Anderson and was well acquainted with his father, Dr. Donald B. Anderson, who had served as head of the Division of Biological Sciences and as Dean of the Graduate School at NC State University while I was there," Colvard said. Anderson later became Bill Friday's vice president for academic affairs.

In the fall of 1970, Robert Anderson announced to architects across the state that the new program would be offered beginning in September 1971. By the start of 1971, Anderson had succeeded in receiving approval for establishing a National Advisory Committee consisting of H. Samuel Kruse of Miami, national commissioner of educational research for the AIA and a visiting professor of architecture at the University of Waterloo in Ontario, Canada; David A. Crane of Philadelphia, a member of the National Architectural Accrediting Board, Inc., and a visiting professor in the Department of Urban Design at the University of Pennsylvania; and Richard D. Barry, an associate professor of architecture at the University of Southern California.

The new school opened in the fall of 1971 with its first freshman class of forty-five, and by the fall of 1972 it had seventy-four students. Colvard noted in a letter to Ferebee on January 13, 1971, that the architects themselves were largely responsible for the creation of the school. "The scarcity of office, laboratory and classroom facilities on the new campus required improvising, rearrangement and crowding each time a new activity was added," Colvard recalled. "For several years the division of education, the college book and supply store and the new program in architecture used space originally built for the library. The creation of the College of Architecture at UNCC occurred under circumstances that may be regarded as unusual in at least two ways: it had the unanimous political support of professional architects from all parts of the state and it was strongly advocated by the dean and chancellor of what might normally be regarded as a competing campus of the same university system. This can be regarded as a display of unselfish educational statesmanship."

14 CREATING AN URBAN INSTITUTE

Despite the calm tone that Colvard kept in his diary, he had lived through a tumultuous time since returning to North Carolina. He had taken a job as the first chancellor of the fourth campus of the University of North Carolina only to find himself serving as the chief executive of one of sixteen campuses in the system. Five years later he was still struggling with the very real challenge of finding key officials and professors to help him build UNCC into the urban-oriented university he had envisioned. But he also knew that he needed some time for rest and recuperation to reflect on the next seven years he would be able to serve before mandatory retirement at the age of sixty-five.

So when officials at the Danforth Foundation offered him a two-month sabbatical, he decided to take it at the University of Hawaii, noting in his diary: "A minimum requirement was that I be away from the office for at least two months and write a two-page report. The sabbatical was based on the proposition that as a general rule chief administrative officers of universities are not able to take full vacations and need some periods of physical and intellectual refurbishment."

He and Martha left for the islands on January 3, 1972. Colvard's sabbatical in Hawaii proved to be exactly what he and Martha needed. Martha became well informed on the plants and birds of the islands. Although he had an office provided for him at the University of Hawaii and he did participate in some seminars at the East-West Conference Center, mostly he and his wife played a lot of golf, ate a lot of exotic food, and traveled about the islands *ooh*ing and *aah*ing over the exotic scenery. "We were free to play golf whenever we wished, to read to our hearts' content and to travel to all of the islands," Colvard noted in his diary. For two glorious months, the problems of running a major university were forgotten. He had never spent more than two weeks away from work in his forty-three-year career. But soon it was time to return home. He and Martha left on March 1 on Northwest Airlines Flight 88 bound for Seattle, where they stayed for a few days, and then flew on to Charlotte.

Colvard returned to a student body of 4,480, a growing faculty, and the university's first board of trustees, headed by Addison Reese, a tough-minded Charlotte banker who was determined to see that UNCC got a fair shake in the General Assembly.

A native of Baltimore, Maryland, Reese had come to Charlotte in the 1950s to make a career in banking. He had started working on building a university for Charlotte in 1957, according to a UNCC oral history interview he gave to Charlotte writer LeGette Blythe in 1970. Reese knew that one of the keys to gaining approval was making sure the university had an appropriate location, not only in size but also in geographic proximity to surrounding residents, potential students. He also knew that two hundred acres were available just north of Charlotte on Highway 49. The land had been used for a county home, a relic of the past where indigent senior citizens were placed to live out their days. "We generally knew that the county was going out of business of operating what used to be known as the 'poor farm' and putting its property to other use," Reese said. "What better use could it possibly be put to than a much needed four-year-college for this county and this area?"

Reese was named vice chairman of the board of trustees of the old Charlotte College in 1963 and became chairman the next year upon the untimely death of Murrey Atkins. Reese said UNCC was behind only his wife and his bank in importance to him. In a September 22, 1964, speech to a group called Friends of Higher Education in the library auditorium at the old Charlotte College, he said that the fourth campus was an urgent necessity. "All of dynamic North Carolina is undergoing change that makes a fourth university campus a social and industrial necessity," Reese said. "Nowhere in the state is the need more apparent now—nor will it be in the foreseeable future—than in our area of immediate accessibility."

In his interview with Blythe, Reese said he and the other UNCC backers decided to make their push for university status during the 1965 legislative session, knowing full well that their chances were slim. "The only hope we had was to make it a part of [Governor Dan Moore's] legislative program as the legislature convened, which he did," Reese recalled. "There was a great deal of debate, a lot of objection on the part of the old line conservatives in the General Assembly." Reese said he knew that the Charlotte area's growth would really develop once the four-year university was established. "I would say that the development of the University of North Carolina at Charlotte is equivalent to the coming of the first railroads," he said. "It was more important than the establishment of the Federal Reserve Bank. It is probably one of the most important developments that has ever taken place in the history of Mecklenburg County." Reese's bank also was responsible for putting the first money into the new nonprofit foundation of UNCC to support the development of the school. "Dean Colvard, the chancellor, is really responsible for the idea of forming what they call the Patrons of Excellence and getting the first 100 Founding Patrons of Excellence," Reese said.

For his part, Colvard had pointed out when he launched the program on November 4, 1966, in a speech at Myers Park Country Club in Charlotte, that no great university had developed without private funds to accompany public ones. As examples, he mentioned the Morehead Scholarships and the Kenan Professorships at UNC Chapel Hill, the Reynolds Distinguished Professors at Wake Forest University and NC State, and others.

"Ours is the peculiar task of building a new university of quality," Colvard had said, "without the immediate help of alumni and of taking our place in a family of distinguished institutions without waiting for three-quarters of a century or a century and three-quarters, as the case may be, to provide us the patrimony our sister institutions possess."

The state legislature was being asked to provide basic support, but private assistance would be needed if UNCC was to achieve greatness, Colvard said. Founding Patrons of Excellence at the university would be asked to give a minimum of $10,000 over a period of ten years. (Colvard and his wife were among the first to commit.) He said the money would be used "to recruit and hold competent faculty members, to encourage and support the beginning of a research program, to strengthen the library and to do some of those first things most necessary to the building of a first-rate institution." A year later, the Patrons of Excellence Program had gathered a total of $1 million in pledges. At a special dinner honoring the first seventy founding members, Colvard said, "I am more convinced than ever that in terms of the need for its services and the opportunity for its success, there is no better place in America to build a university than here."

Another Colvard initiative was the Institute for Urban Studies and Community Service. It had been a dream of his since the beginning of UNCC, when he had sought separate funding just for what he called the Urban Information Center. In September 1968, he had told the North Carolina General Assembly that the center was needed to help solve "some of the nation's great urban problems." The center would be charged with finding ways to "help this new university to respond to the needs of today and to become involved appropriately in training, research, and public service as means of seeking solutions to these problems."

Charlotte-Mecklenburg planning director William E. McIntyre saw the potential for such an urban institute in Charlotte at an early stage. In May 19, 1966, responding to a request for his endorsement, he said, "We have an unusual opportunity here to fashion an urban structure in the Piedmont region that would avoid many of the appalling problems found in the massive urban agglomerations in the northeast and on the west coast. This will be done, of course, only if we have understanding of the problems and opportunities that confront us. . . . the university could play a vital role in helping to enlighten this area and the state in desirable policies and objectives in regional urbanization." In a meeting hosted by Knight Publishing Company of Charlotte on December 4, 1969, Colvard said, "From the beginning, urban affairs has been regarded as a major commitment. . . . Our purpose is to make life in the city one of enrichment and fulfillment."

Through a series of urban seminars and conferences dealing with the future of the Piedmont Crescent and through many committee activities involving faculty and leaders in the community, a basis was established for submitting a request to the 1969 legislature for funds to establish a center for urban studies. The proposal had the endorsement of President Friday, governors Moore and Scott, the UNC Board of Trustees, and members of the Mecklenburg County legislative delegation. The request for $500,000 was approved and sent to the UNC administration. But UNCC received only $85,165. Colvard did not let the setback reduce the commitment to urban affairs at Charlotte. Although it slowed the process, it also stimulated the new institute to seek funds by furnishing consultant activity with local governments and others to help fulfill its mission. Over time the funds from the central command in Chapel Hill increased sufficiently until the institute's operating budget was reasonably adequate. The director's salary had to be acquired from various sources within the UNC Charlotte budget. The director position was one of those that Colvard had hoped might be appropriated directly by the legislature.

The Institute for Urban Studies and Community Service was officially launched in 1970 under the leadership of Dr. Norman W. Schul, a Ph.D. in geography from Syracuse University who came to UNCC from UNC Greensboro. During the institute's first year, a full-time conference coordinator was added to the staff to assist in eighteen seminars, institutes, and workshops. Programs included a census users' workshop, a clear air workshop, the "Who Shall Live?" seminar, an urban affairs advisory conference, the Robert A. Taft Institute of Government seminar, and three general sessions of the Piedmont Urban Policy Conference, which studied various problems in the area. The institute supported research dealing with city-county consolidation for Charlotte-Mecklenburg County, pathogenic bacteria in urban waste, mental health in the inner city, and the preparation of a land policy bibliography for the North Carolina state planning division.

In the next academic year, 1971–72, the institute sponsored two first-rate publications—the *Metrolina Atlas*, by Drs. James W. Clay and Douglas M. Orr, Jr., and *Citizen Attitudes and Metropolitan Government: City-County Consolidation in Charlotte*, by Dr. Schley R. Lyons. Lyons also headed the Department of Political Science. He came to UNCC from the University of Toledo, where he was acting director of the Urban Studies Center as well as a member of the political science department. Lyons received his B.S. and B.A. from Shepherd College and his Ph.D. from American University.

Some of the programs were considered ambitious for their time, such as the one between the institute and the Charlotte Area Fund offering a fifteen-month-long training program to welfare recipients with the goal of improving their self-images. "People who entered the program with a good deal of skepticism and anxiety became more confident, self-assured and able to deal with situations they would not have attempted earlier," according to the institute's 1972–73 annual report.

Over the years, the institute assisted local governments in a wide range of consultant activities, ranging from studies on the environment to land-use mapping. The National Science Foundation funded institute programs to help high-ability high school students understand urban problems. The institute also produced a series of guidebooks on revitalization of downtown retailing, promoting a revitalized downtown, architectural and planning considerations, and federal funding sources.

With the Urban Institute firmly established, Colvard could turn his mind to other important matters. But he was struck a blow when Hugh McEniry, who had returned from Western Carolina, suddenly died. The following recruitment showed again Colvard's resourcefulness in attracting national names to help build a university out of nothing. Colvard quickly turned his attention to recruiting another strong academic leader, and he found one in the person of Dr. Frank G. Dickey, fifty-seven, who was director of the National Commission on Accrediting of Colleges and Universities in Washington, D.C. "I needed someone who had great experience in educational administration and who could help lead this young faculty," Colvard recalled. "Dickey was the perfect candidate, and he certainly was well qualified. He had visited more campuses than anyone I knew." A native of Oklahoma, Dickey had received his undergraduate education at Transylvania College in Kentucky and his M.A. and Ph.D. in education from the University of Kentucky. After teaching in the university's College of Education and becoming its dean, he was named president of the university in 1956 at the age of thirty-eight, the youngest president in the institution's history.

He served as president until 1963, when he became director of the Southern Association of Colleges and Schools, where he stayed until 1965 when he took the job supervising the National Commission on Accrediting. When Colvard approached him in early 1974, Dickey had decided to seek a new job by July 1, 1974, when the National Commission on Accrediting that he was heading would merge with the Federation of Regional Accrediting Commissions in Higher Education. He and Colvard had known each other since the 1950s and had become closer friends in the early 1960s, when Colvard was president of Mississippi State and Dickey was president at Kentucky as well as president of the Southeastern Conference. Colvard had invited him to Mississippi State to deliver a commencement address and he had kept up with him over the years, so when he heard that Dickey might be looking for a job, he immediately called upon him in Washington, since Miller was gone and Hugh McEniry had died. "Working with Dean was a delightful experience," Dickey recalled in a July 2003 interview. "I have never seen him flustered by anything. He is always calm and collected."

Colvard eventually succeeded in having the new post of provost created to accommodate Dickey's arrival at UNCC. As second in command at the campus, Dickey was in charge of all day-to-day administrative details. When Colvard was away in China in 1975, Dickey hired the new basketball coach Lee Rose without any input from the chancellor. Colvard learned about it when he read newspapers on the West Coast upon his return. Dickey stayed at UNCC as provost until 1976, when he left to become a consultant in higher education in Washington. "I felt the things I had come to Charlotte to do were well under way and I didn't have any hesitancy about leaving at that point," Dickey recalled.

15

A GOVERNOR'S OFFER

In the fall of 1976, Colvard received a pleasant surprise when one of his former students at NC State was elected to the state's highest office. James B. Hunt had been studying animal husbandry and then switched to agriculture education under Colvard's deanship in the School of Agriculture. He had graduated, gone on to law school at UNC Chapel Hill, and returned to Wilson, where he practiced law until being elected lieutenant governor in 1972.

Hunt remembered his former dean fondly and respected his judgment and administrative abilities so much that when he was elected governor in 1976 he offered Colvard a job as his top executive assistant. "Here I was a brand-new elected governor, only thirty-six years old," Hunt explained. "I needed to have a mature, seasoned person with strong administrative skills and good people skills to help me run the governor's office and be governor of North Carolina."

Hunt recalled the time that he had gone to Colvard for advice when Hunt was editor of a student magazine at NC State. He had written an editorial criticizing Governor Luther Hodges for appointing industrialist B. Everett Jordan to the U.S. Senate seat left vacant by the death of W. Kerr Scott, a former state commissioner of agriculture and a champion of the farmer. "He didn't say, 'Don't run it,'" Hunt said. "He shared with me some of the things that Governor Hodges was doing to work with the university and the school of agriculture, that he thought we were making progress and that Hodges meant well for the school. I went home and thought it over and finally decided that maybe it was best not to run that editorial."

In late November 1976, Hunt's office called to ask Colvard to come to Raleigh to discuss a possible job in the new administration. He and Hunt met in room 220 of the Hilton Inn in Raleigh. "He said if I would join him I would become his number one appointment and would be in charge of his office in his absence," Colvard recalled. "He indicated he would want me to be the principal contact with his office for his appointed heads of agencies." The salary was to be $28,000, less than I was making at UNC Charlotte, but salary wasn't the problem. After discussing the matter with Martha and with Addison Reese, who was chairman of the board of trustees at Charlotte, and thinking about it a great deal more myself, I decided this was a bad time for me to leave UNC Charlotte." Reese was adamantly opposed because he felt losing Colvard would slow UNCC's progress, and the university was in the midst of changing the heads of four departments.

Years later Colvard said he realized that he had passed up a great opportunity, but that he never regretted his decision. He felt obligated to continue to try to build UNC Charlotte, and he also realized that taking the job with Hunt would have required total political commitment. Hunt was disappointed, but said he understood why Colvard had to stay in Charlotte.

Basketball, which had played such an important part of Colvard's life at Mississippi State, emerged as one of the highlights of his career at UNCC. In 1969, he finally found a way to hire a highly qualified coach in the person of Bill Foster. An assistant coach at the Citadel, Foster had coached at Shorter College in Rome, Georgia, where he had winning teams during the six seasons when he was the head coach. "We gave him a year to recruit before he took over the team," Colvard said. Meanwhile, the team continued to be coached by Harvey Murphy. There was no money in the university's budget to pay Foster's salary, so Colvard had to dip into the university union's activity funds.

The beginning of Foster's era coincided with UNC Charlotte's moving into the NCAA beginning with the 1970–71 season. Foster's first year at Charlotte resulted in a 15-8 record, but no national recognition. The second year the team went 14-11 and the third, 1973–74, improved to 22-4, but still no bid from the NCAA for postseason play. The team went 23-3 in 1974–75, and still no bid. After that season, Foster left to become the head coach at Clemson University, and Colvard approved the hiring of Lee Rose as his successor. Rose had been head coach at

Transylvania College in Lexington, Kentucky, where he had racked up a 160-57 record in eight years.

In his first year at Charlotte, Rose's team went 21-5. The NCAA again failed to offer a bid, but one did come from the National Invitational Tournament in New York City. Although it lost to Kentucky 67-71 in the final game, UNC Charlotte was suddenly on the national map. Its star, Cedric "Cornbread" Maxwell, was named most valuable player of the tournament. "Nobody thought we would be able to field a high-caliber team," Colvard recalled. "But they soon found out that UNC Charlotte was a national contender." Colvard shuttled back and forth to New York on a private plane carrying books for the players, who had not been expected to stay a week.

The university received its first NCAA bid the following year, when the team defeated first Central Michigan, then Syracuse, and a strong University of Michigan team, which was ranked number one in the nation, before reaching the Final Four, where UNCC lost to Marquette.

By the time he retired in December 1978, Colvard could point to many other accomplishments during his twelve years as the university's chief executive, including the University Research Park, which was modeled after the Research Triangle Park in Raleigh. (He co-authored a book about the history of that project.) Charlotte banker C. C. Cameron, who had succeeded Reese as chairman of the UNCC board and worked well with Colvard, was a driving force in the establishment of the research center.

In his last report to President Bill Friday and the Board of Governors of the university, Colvard said, "In this my thirteenth and final annual report as chancellor of the University of North Carolina at Charlotte, I am pleased to be able to report that the institution has reached a level of academic excellence and attainment at which I can turn over the reins to a new leader with a sense of accomplishment and a feeling of gratitude to those who made the achievements here possible." He listed the growth from 1966 to 1978: enrollment increased from 1,715 students to 8,504; undergraduate degree programs from eighteen to thirty-four; graduate programs from zero to ten; the number of volumes in the library from 60,000 to 275,000; the value of the physical plant from $8.1 million to more than $54 million; the square footage in use or under construction from 355,633 to 1,557,313, with another seven buildings with 211,995 square feet authorized; and full-time faculty from 99 to 378, with 85 percent holding doctoral degrees.

Colvard's report also noted the "extension of the geographic reach of the institution from Mecklenburg and immediately surrounding counties to 88 of the state's counties last year along with students from 30 states." And he added that the number of alumni had grown from a handful to more than 13,000. "All these improvements speak of growth and development," Colvard said, "but the ultimate yardstick for measuring quality is the success of the University's graduates. In areas where graduates take professional or state licensing examinations, UNCC's graduates perform with the best the state has to offer. Significantly, they perform well in graduate schools and in a wide range of employment."

Colvard, who had directed an annual budget that had grown to $18.6 million, could point with pride to other accomplishments as well. The UNCC Foundation's assets had grown to $2,517,116. Endowments held directly by the university totaled $677,460 and trusts that would accrue to it were more than $850,000. A total of 197 individuals or organizations had become Patrons of Excellence, donating or pledging a minimum of $1,000 per year for ten years. The University Research Park had attracted such occupants as Allstate, Collins & Aikman, Reeves Brothers, and IBM. Friends and supporters had pledged $375,000 for the Dean and Martha Colvard Merit Scholarship Fund.

"I am proud indeed of the progress resulting from the efforts of so many people," Colvard concluded, "but I would be remiss if I did not point to the needs remaining after my departure. These include the need to:

"1. Narrow the gap between the level of salaries of UNCC and other major universities.
"2. Continue to provide for the physical needs brought about by growth.
"3. Continue and increase support for the library.
"4. Provide essential administrative and staff positions.
"5. Expand and strengthen the area of urban affairs research and service.
"6. Remove some administrative positions currently funded out of academic budgets and fund them properly as administrative positions.

"Despite these needs, I am unwavering in my faith in the future of this institution. My successor will encounter a strong academic base which derives from the strength of the faculty and the experiences—both successes and failures which have marked the first 12 years. To the extent my services are needed following retirement they will be available on call. I remain grateful for a personally rewarding career and I am irrevocably committed to the development of UNCC into an institution that realizes great potential in education and service."

Colvard wrote in his diary, "There was a time when I had begun to wonder if I would ever enjoy the warm and trusting relations at UNCC similar to what I had experienced at NC State and Mississippi State. Indeed I do feel that my work has been appreciated and that my administration has been characterized by integrity and progress."

16 RETIREMENT

Dean Colvard was nearly as busy in retirement as he had been for the previous forty-three years. He was asked to take on a variety of civic and charitable roles, including chairmanship of the creation of the North Carolina School of Science and Mathematics in Durham in 1979. Governor Jim Hunt, who had asked Colvard to be his executive assistant when he won his first term in 1976, sought out Colvard for this important role. "I chose him because of his vision and the respect in which he was held in North Carolina, which meant he could bring great respect and support to that new institution," Hunt recalled. "We needed to have a superb and highly respected chairman of the board to get it under way and to make sure it was built to be the kind of institution with the impact we wanted to have in North Carolina and nationally."

Hunt appointed Colvard to the Southern Growth Policies Board, which helps set policies for economic growth in North Carolina and other southern states. "He spent his life trying to build the economy, working primarily in agriculture and agribusiness and related areas, which is still the largest single industry in this state," Hunt said. "But also he had this feel for the land and he was a conservationist both in practice and in his heart. He always wanted to be sure we did things right, that we were good stewards and so he was a marvelous representative of North Carolina." Hunt also named Colvard to a panel to help select superior court judges in the western part of the state.

One of Colvard's most challenging volunteer posts came in 1980, when Charlotte was getting ready to open a new science museum. Charlotte voters had approved $7.1 million in bond money to buy the land and construct the building and work was already under way. "My initial reaction was that it was a worthy community project and that I would like to help," Colvard recalled. The museum's trustees offered him a salary of $35,000 per year to head the museum, but he turned it down, preferring to work without pay.

One of his first moves in working on the project was the unpleasant task of having to inform the man who had worked so hard to make the museum possible that he was no longer needed. "Before we had proceeded very far I found that it was going to be necessary to relieve the person who had the dream of Discovery Place from his responsibilities and to replace him with an acting director of that unit," Colvard recalled.

After several months of working with the museum's staff, Colvard came to admire the ability of the museum's health director, Freda Nicholson, and talked her into assuming the job of acting director. Eventually, she was hired as the first full-time director of Discovery Place and served until her retirement. "Freda took over and very quickly became one of the most highly respected leaders in the field of scientific museum administration," Colvard said. "I considered this one of my most successful post-retirement assignments. In retrospect, this assignment represents my style of administration in attempting to let sound procedures emerge by bringing principal actors together on a project of which I had relatively little knowledge." He called it the "organic process."

After retirement Colvard authored or coauthored three documentary books. The first was *Mixed Emotions: A University President Remembers*, published by the Interstate Printers and Publishers, Inc., of Evansville, Illinois, dealing with his civil rights experiences while president of Mississippi State University. The second was *Knowledge Is Power*, coauthored with Dr. William Carpenter, covering the history of the School of Agriculture and Life Sciences at NC State University and published by NC State. The third was *University Research Park: The First Twenty Years*, coauthored with Dr. Douglas Orr and Mary Dawn Bailey and published by the University Research Park. He also wrote an unpublished autobiography for his family covering his life until his arrival at UNC Charlotte.

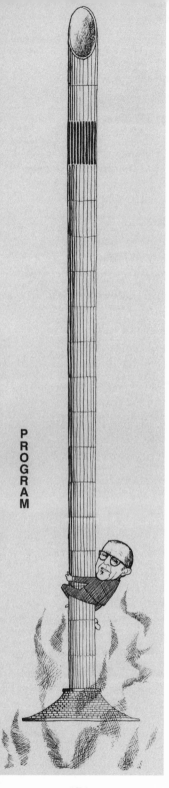

P
R
O
G
R
A
M

From left: Dean Colvard, Addison Reese, Chairman of the University of North Carolina at Charlotte Foundation Trustees, and Governor Dan K. Moore.

From left: C. C. Cameron, Chairman of the Trustees, Dean Colvard, Martha Colvard, and Harold Warren of the *Charlotte Observer,* as Colvard announces his retirement, 1978.

From left: Harry Dalton, Dean Colvard, C. C. Cameron, Chairman of the Trustees, and Ty Boyd, emcee, at Colvard's retirement roast dinner, April 7, 1978.

At left: Retirement roast dinner invitation cover art

174

This group involved in planning and launching the Research Triangle met at Governor's Inn on May 30, 1986, to discuss plans to write the history of the Triangle.

University of North Carolina President Frank Porter Graham (left) receives the first honorary degree at University of North Carolina at Charlotte, 1968.

John Paul Lucas, former trustee of Charlotte College; member of Board of Higher Education; recipient of honorary degree, 1969.

175

University of North Carolina President C. D. Spangler poses with the 1989 recipients of the University of North Carolina Award. Three UNC campuses were represented. From left: Leroy Walker of North Carolina Central University, Dean Colvard of UNC Charlotte, Spangler, and John Caldwell of North Carolina State University.

Dean Colvard (left) and N.C. Agricultural Commisioner James A. Graham. The two were first and second directors of the Upper Mountain Research Station. 1996.

Good friends Dean Colvard (left) and Harry Dalton, 1984.

From left: Dean and Martha Colvard, Francena and Paul Miller, and E. K. Fretwell, October 28, 1996.

From left: C. D. Spangler, Chancellor James H. Woodward, Bonnie Cone, Bill Friday, Dean Colvard, and E. K. Fretwell launch a new campaign, 2000.

Bill Friday (left) and Dean Colvard at the dedication of the Lee College of Engineering at North Carolina State University, November 1, 1994.

Martha and Dean Colvard at Dean's cousin's (Edie Colvard Crutcher) Ashe County home, June 2000.

Dean Colvard (left) with James B. Hunt at the dedication of the Butler Building at North Carolina State University, 2002.

17 TRIBUTES AND HONORS

The view to the west from the highest point on the UNCC campus reminds one of the scenery around Grassy Creek in the mountains of North Carolina where Dean Colvard spent his boyhood. Rolling hills, tall trees, and lush greenery spread out in a peaceful panorama. Dean Colvard was right at home in both places. In the mountains, he learned self-sufficiency and the basic goodness of men and women, regardless of their skin color. He learned the value of honesty, modesty, and hard work, lots of hard work. Nothing came easy in the mountains, whether it was trying to trap enough rabbits to earn some spending money or putting up a barn for your neighbors.

The same was true of Dean Colvard's tenure as the first outsider to become president of Mississippi State University and the first chancellor of the brand-new fourth campus of the University of North Carolina. Soon after taking on the assignment he was told that he would be leading one of sixteen campuses, but he was not discouraged by the news, interpreting it only as another challenge to be overcome. He had to be an astute faculty recruiter with only low salaries to offer instead of a prestigious institution with years of tradition. He had to be an outstanding fund-raiser, community builder, hands-on administrator, and hard worker. Every day seemed to bring a new challenge. First he had to try to encourage a tightfisted legislature to part with enough money to set a true course for the fledging university. Craftily he appealed to private foundations for enough seed money to try to establish his new university as a national leader in planning for an urban setting. He had to fight the prejudice against the neophyte institution that was exhibited time after time when some legislators and other political leaders, mostly in Raleigh, would bypass UNCC in favor of their alma maters at UNC Chapel Hill or NC State. The local institution was almost like an afterthought, and since there was no large number of influential alumni to stem the flow of sentimentality and donations, UNCC, with Colvard at the helm, had to work hard to prove itself worthy. He had to fight local prejudice from some business leaders who thought the new campus should have been downtown and felt that it was too far out of town, regardless of the fact that it was only nine miles from the city center.

In addition to his regular duties, which would have been tough enough for three capable administrators, Colvard encountered other drawbacks. First, there was a critical lack of water on campus. Then there were elevators that refused to work, faculty members who were constantly attempting to challenge the system, the normal spates of student unrest, and on and on and on.

He had to be a man of infinite patience, and he was. And he was extraordinarily supportive of his people. "While a lot of chancellors make it on charisma and force of magnetic personality, he made it on intellect," said Dennis Rash, Colvard's dean of students in the early 1970s. "He has made it by putting really deep roots in the ground. He's thoughtful. He has a remarkable ability at assessing human potential. I can't tell you how many times he could look at an individual and see that the individual had potential for growth or did not."

Rash remembered fondly how Colvard had backed him when Rash ordered the elevator shut down for weeks to all eleven floors of a dorm when unknown students kept rewiring it as a prank. (A student finally confessed to the stunt, and Rash turned the elevators back on.)

Dr. Norman Schul was only thirty-three when Colvard recruited him from UNC Greensboro to become UNCC's first director of the Institute for Urban Studies and Community Service. "I was really taken aback by the man," Schul said. "We hit it off immediately. He basically said, 'Look, I believe in the organic process. I want to bring people here who can bring their talents and begin to shape a university that is different from other universities." In the many years Schul worked for Colvard as director of the institute and in other posts, the two never clashed. "I felt he was a man I could trust," Schul said. "He would let me do what I set out to do without interfering. He told me that if I wasn't doing the job he would let me know, but never once did he criticize me in all the years I spent with him."

Colvard found himself with a very young faculty and staff, primarily because he couldn't afford to lure top, experienced people away from other prestigious colleges and universities, and because UNCC was so young that many in the academic community had never heard of it. Dennis Rash is a case in point. He was a young lawyer in Charlotte with no experience in academia when Colvard convinced him to leave the law and come to UNCC as dean of students at the age of thirty. "I had done a lot of youth work at the First Presbyterian Church and our pastor, Lee Stoffel, knew Dean was looking for a dean of students," Rash recalled. "So Lee arranged for me to meet Dr. Colvard as a way of addressing the question of whether there was another career path that would keep me in Charlotte. What wasn't known was that I had a remarkable opportunity to found a practice in Boone." Rash was impressed with Colvard's sincerity and bought into his sense of mission to have UNCC become a leading university. "He said and I agreed how important it would be to the future of Charlotte to have a vibrant university here. He was remarkably skillful at conveying that kind of institutional destiny."

Former UNC system president Bill Friday, the man who chose Colvard to become UNCC's first chancellor, said, "He is a man of integrity and courage and high energy. There were other people but he was the only person I went after. A part of picking Dean Colvard is Martha. She is an absolutely superior woman who understood that a wife of a chancellor has to be very much into the work of the institution and into making people feel at home. We got two for one there."

Friday said he had been friends with Colvard since Colvard was a professor and then dean at NC State back in the 1950s. "The emergence of UNCC at the time of that chancellor selection was such that everyone knew that we had to move the institution on into the doctoral level of consideration," Friday said. "That is, you had to have in motion plans to create a very mature university there, meaning all the normal and traditional offerings of baccalaureate, master's and doctorate training plus a lot of collateral institutes. That said we had to have somebody who had widespread experience. I knew first hand of what D. W. [Colvard] had done at Raleigh and I had kept up with what he was doing at Mississippi State and he became the very logical person to bring home. This was because of his vast skill in building a curriculum and measuring everything qualitatively. The committee was unanimous for him. That made it easy for me. All I had to do was talk him into coming home." Colvard's great strengths were his systematic approach to solving problems and his professionalism, Friday added.

Dr. Dan Morrill was a twenty-eight-year-old history professor at UNCC when Colvard arrived at the university in 1966. "He brought a sense of legitimacy, a sense of having arrived because he was a man who had already held the presidency [of Mississippi State]," Morrill said years later. "He had a background at North Carolina State. He was someone who was a known figure in the Consolidated University [of North Carolina]. He is very proper, controlled, cautious, but also a man in the bigger picture who took a tremendous gamble by coming to what was then an institution that some people thought wasn't going to make it. It was not at all a sure thing when he came." Morrill came to what was then Charlotte College in 1963 just after having received his doctorate degree from Emory University. He remembered that there was apprehension among the faculty when it was announced that Colvard was going to be the first chancellor. "There was a flicker of resentment over the fact that Bonnie Cone was being asked to step aside," Morrill said. "There were questions. 'Who is this guy? He's going to come in here and think that everything we have done is minor league and he's going to do everything over.'" But Colvard soon won over the faculty, he said, and proved that he was a very efficient administrator and brought a team spirit as a known factor in the university system. "At a roast for him, I kidded him by saying, 'To think I came to an urban university with a chancellor who came from Grassy Creek,'" Morrill said.

Colvard had his critics among some faculty members who believed that he wasn't enough of a fighter, that he didn't stand up enough for the university, Morrill and others have said, but that criticism faded as the institution grew and it became clear that it ranked among the best the system had to offer. "He's not a backslapper. He's not a hugger. He wasn't an ebullient personality, but I never doubted his power and his strength," Morrill said. "He is a man of great integrity. Dr. Colvard is a gentleman and a man of great compassion, but if you put him in a corner he's tough as nails. There's an iron fist in that velvet glove." Morrill recalled being one of the young professors who pushed for public disclosure of faculty salaries at UNCC when Colvard disagreed. "I remember he reminded me kind of a Robert E. Lee. He could be very firm." Morrill said Colvard's legacy at UNCC included a mature university, the Institute for Urban Studies and Community Service, and the University Research Park.

Cliff Cameron, former chairman of First Union Corporation and chairman of the UNCC Board of Trustees in 1977, said, "Dean was absolutely the right person at the right time. He was perfect. He not only had experience as a dean at NC State University, but he had experience as a president at Mississippi State University. We were so fortunate. I assume it was Bill Friday's relationship with Dean that enticed him to come back to a little beginning university, leaving a good job at Mississippi State University to take on building the University of North Carolina at Charlotte. He was a proven manager, executive, leader, that was required to build almost from the ground up a new university. You see a lot of Dean Colvard is in that university today. He was the guy that set the patterns, that built the foundation for it to grow on."

Commenting on Colvard's management style, Cameron said, "I wouldn't describe him as an aggressive person, but one that was a dedicated, hands-on-type executive that surrounded himself with good people that could bring that university from nothing to really a prominent institution now. He was never a showman. He was always reserved, almost an introvert, certainly not an extrovert, but had that ability to select the right people and get them to perform. He's a good listener. That's always a sign of great executive in my opinion. He's quietly efficient." A person of Colvard's experience and background was needed to overcome all the problems connected with building UNCC, Cameron said. "It would have been tough for somebody else to perform with a little institution that was located in Mecklenburg County that as the people in the east have always thought of as the Great State of Mecklenburg. They thought Charlotte didn't need any help. We had a tough time back in those early days. The fact of that very close tie between Bill Friday and Dean Colvard was the great success story in the beginning."

Dr. Douglas M. Orr, Jr., was fresh from having defended his Ph.D. thesis in geography at UNC Chapel Hill in the winter of 1968 when he was interviewed by Colvard for a faculty position to teach geography. He was told that no money was available for the job, but asked if he would be interested in becoming Colvard's administrative assistant, and he jumped at the chance. "I saw UNCC as an institution of the future and I was really interested in getting in on the ground floor," Orr said. He stayed at UNCC in various jobs, including vice chancellor of student affairs, until 1991, when he became president of Warren Wilson College in Swannanoa, just east of Asheville. "We were always stretched to the limit [at UNCC]," he recalled. "It was almost as if the university was on fast forward with never the resource base to start a new university, but simply being declared part of the university system and then having to find, by hook or crook, resources to keep up with the dramatic enrollment growth."

Despite the lack of resources, UNCC was being considered a new model for urban universities throughout the nation. "Oftentimes we would have to take academic money just to fund an administrative position," Orr recalled.

One of the problems Colvard had to deal with was the high level of expectation from the young faculty members. "There was probably a higher expectation that with the president of Mississippi State University coming in that we were going to have instant credibility," Orr said. "But it still took years of grinding away. Like at East Carolina University, there was a hunger for recognition. It was hard to move from the perception of Charlotte College to the university level." Colvard had the perfect attitude to do that job, Orr said. "There was a steeliness in him that he was not going to be deterred. He never complained, never talked about having less resources than was required. We are given credit for carrying out the urban university concept, but in many ways we were simply carrying out Dean's vision."

Colvard wasn't all seriousness. Orr said his boss at UNCC loved to tell the story of how his geography-trained assistant got lost. "He had planned an executive staff retreat at Montreat in the mountains. He had all the rooms reserved and wanted me to be there to hand out the keys to everybody else. Unfortunately two of the deans and I decided to take a shortcut from Charlotte. I was driving. We got on some country roads and got totally lost. We got there about forty-five minutes after everybody else. Dean loves to tell that story."

Dr. Ben Romine, who later served as Colvard's director of the Office of Academic Planning and Institutional Research, recalled his first interview with Colvard. "I said, 'You've got some really good things going here. I can imagine how excited you are, but you've got some problems.' At that point I saw his eyebrows lift up and he leaned over and said kindly, 'Dr. Romine, we know we have some problems. We're looking for people to help us solve them.'" Colvard's stoicism was legendary, Romine said. "He always kept a reserve. He was not a dreamer. He would never sit down with his hands behind his head and put his feet up on the desk. He talked about doing things, getting this funded and how that might happen. It was his style to get these good people together and let *them* dream."

Colvard's genius was to act as a catalyst rather than a charismatic leader. "He was steady, contemplative—didn't overreact, but listened," Romine said. "Then he would make a decision and you knew a decision had been made. There was no wishy-washiness about it. It may be unpopular, but it had been carefully considered." Colvard had no rigid set of goals in mind for the university, Romine said. Since it was not Chapel Hill or NC State or even Mississippi State, Colvard was having to shape UNCC into whatever it would become. "He would bring the personnel and resources together and let things bubble up," Romine said. Colvard had to contend with not only normal problems in higher education, but since the legislative funding was based upon enrollment and UNCC was growing so fast, it was always struggling to keep up with its growth. "The funding was always two years behind," Romine said.

UNCC is still coming into its own, but the shape it has taken must be laid at the feet of Dean Colvard, Romine and others agree. Over and over Colvard exhibited courage in the face of pressure. On one occasion, a powerful politician came to Colvard and asked him to bypass the normal channels and enroll his son at UNCC, despite the fact that the son's grades were below admission standards. "He [the politician] even told him that that was how Leo Jenkins was able to curry favor at East Carolina, by admitting students that political leaders asked him to," Romine said.

Colvard turned down the request and wrote in his diary on November 20, 1970, "Today I was shocked by a visit from [state] Sen. ——— to tell me that we should admit anybody recommended by a member of the legislature. He said that if we expect favors from legislators we must do favors for them—independent of our admission standards. He said Leo Jenkins did this and if we expected results we would have to do likewise. He used Jenkins' recruitment for his daughter who had low academic standards as an example. I had to tell him that before I would operate that way I would resign."

The politician went away empty-handed and never brought up the subject again. But Colvard had to continue to appear before him on future funding requests, and their relationship was always uncomfortable.

Perhaps former governor Jim Hunt, who once offered Colvard the job as his top executive assistant, gave the best summary of his long and illustrious career. "I consider him to be one of the great men of our time and frankly one of the great men in North Carolina history," Hunt said. Colvard always impressed him as a man of great integrity and clarity of thinking, he said. "Dean Colvard is a man who comes from humble beginnings, who has a deep caring and concern for all human beings," Hunt continued. "He judges them based on their merit and their deeds, not birth or family or position or power. He is really dedicated to helping improve life and giving people opportunities and providing equal opportunities for all human beings. So he's got the right values, but he puts with all that, of course, a great intellect, a driving ambition to improve things, including all these wonderful institutions he's been with, and he works his head off to make it happen."

Dr. E. K. Fretwell, who succeeded Colvard as chancellor at UNCC in 1978, said, "It was like stepping aboard a moving train." Colvard was very helpful, Fretwell said. "He was there to answer questions but he didn't spend time looking over my shoulder. He didn't provide free, unwanted advice. He leads by example." Colvard built a university from modest beginnings against great odds, Fretwell said. "People forget that of the now sixteen campuses, this was number four. This was not a little college in Asheville or Wilmington. Those were Pekinese; this was a bulldog. There was competition and not just for the money. There were no big numbers of rich and powerful alumni, but people rallied around him and realized this was the wave of the future."

Colvard had always enjoyed good health. A clean liver, he was a man of moderation. So it came as a surprise to his close friends when he informed them in 1990 that he was going to go under the knife for a triple heart bypass. His recovery was longer and slower than most of his friends expected. Recognizing this, one of "Colvard's boys," Doug Orr, decided it was time to organize a road trip back to Grassy Creek. He called Dennis Rash, who agreed to bring his wife Betty and accompany Orr and his wife Darcy on the trip with Colvard and his wife Martha.

"We rented the fanciest van we could find," Orr said. "We told Dean, 'All you have to do is tell us where you want us to go next.' We stayed at a great bed and breakfast in the area and just toured around with Dean telling stories about his growing up in Grassy Creek. Not too long after that trip we heard that Dean was back to his old self."

That trip was the first of several annual treks for "Colvard and the boys"—to Charleston, Savannah, Charlottesville, and back to Berea, where they visited the chapel where Dean and Martha were married in 1939.

HONORS

Progressive Farmer Man of the Year in North Carolina Agriculture, 1954.

North Carolina Farm Bureau Distinguished Service Award, 1956.

North Carolina State Grange Man of the Year, 1958.

Mississippi Farm Bureau Meritorious and Outstanding Service Award, 1965.

U.S. Department of the Army Outstanding Civilian Award, 1966.

4-H Alumni Recognition Award, 1970.

Danforth Foundation Sabbatical Grant for University President Recipient, 1972.

Charlotte News Man of the Year, 1977.

Colvard Merit Scholar Fund (as of 2003 more than $1.5 million given by Friends of UNC Charlotte as endowment to provide full scholarships and international travel for outstanding students, named in honor of Martha and Dean Colvard), 1978.

Dean Wallace Colvard classroom/office building at UNC Charlotte, dedicated May 1979.

President, Charlotte Rotary Club, 1978–79.

Berea College Distinguished Alumnus Award, 1980.

North Carolina Association of Colleges and Universities William Hugh McEniry Award, 1981.

Mecklenburg Bar Association Liberty Bell Award, 1982.

Ruling Elder, Covenant Presbyterian Church, Charlotte, North Carolina, 1967–73.

Dean W. Colvard Union Building at Mississippi State University, dedicated April 1985.

Colvard Park (a residential subdivision in Charlotte), dedicated October 31, 1988.

University of North Carolina University Award, 1989.

North Carolina Public Service Award, 1990.

Dean W. Colvard Distinguished Professorship in Nursing, UNC Charlotte, 1991.

Berea College Alumni Loyalty Award, 1993.

Dean W. Colvard Conference Room of the Butler Building at NC State University, dedicated 1999.

UNC Charlotte Alumni by Choice Award, 2001.

Charlotte Echo Award Against Indifference, 2004.

HONORARY DEGREES

Doctor of Agriculture, Purdue University, 1961.
Doctor of Humane Letters, Belmont Abbey College, 1978.
Doctor of Public Service, UNC Charlotte, 1979.
Doctor of Humane Letters Degree, Berea College, 2003

EPILOGUE

NC STATE

Looking back on his life when he was ninety, Colvard said he realized many years later that his management style had been shaped by powerful personalities immediately before and during his days at NC State. "I realize now that I was invited as one of the persons to help Frank Porter Graham realize his dream and the goals of Dr. Clarence Poe and Dr. L. D. Baver of putting NC State in the top ranks of agricultural schools in the nation," Colvard said. "Few people recognize just how large that dream was and how important it was." Graham not only recognized the importance of agriculture education to the academic community, but he could see that research would lead to practical applications for the farmers in the state. It also would enrich farm life and conserve soils and other natural resources. The fast-paced style, attention to detail, and seemingly boundless ambition that Graham embodied rubbed off on Colvard and other young leaders at NC State.

"I was promoted much too fast for my age and experience," Colvard said. "But the forces that were put into motion when I was at State could never be stopped. They fed on each other."

As dean of agriculture at NC State from 1953 to 1960, Colvard recommended twelve of the first fifteen Reynolds Professors. "Most of them spent their entire careers at NC State," he said. "This accumulated collection of diverse intellects coalesced and influenced the university greatly." Colvard also pointed out that the plan to bolster NC State's rank among educational institutions had succeeded immensely as shown in the number of Ph.D.s awarded—from none in 1947 to forty-one by 1960, with thirty-four of those in the College of Agriculture and Life Sciences.

As he celebrated his ninetieth birthday, he proudly showed his guests at the Cypress, a senior center in Charlotte where he and Martha lived, the well-groomed tall fescue lawn and reminded them that this grass was introduced to North Carolina as Kentucky 31 in one of his pasture research projects when he was employed by NC State in 1947.

MISSISSIPPI STATE

Despite their history-making game in 1963, the Mississippi State Bull-dogs did not win enough basketball games the following year to advance to the NCAA tournament. In fact, it would be twenty-eight years before the Bulldogs made it that far again. But when they did reach the NCAA championship level again in 1991, their exploits of 1963 were resuscitated by the national press. "A generation ago, in an era of racial turbulence, the Bulldogs were prohibited three times from going to the NCAA Tournament because they would be playing teams that included blacks," Scripps Howard News Service reporter Thomas O'Toole wrote on March 12, 1991. "Finally, in 1963, the school shook the sports world by standing up to the racial prejudice of some in state government and rallying behind a courageous president who decided to make a bold stand."

The team that MSU sent to play in the 1991 regional at Syracuse, New York, had ten blacks and only three whites on its roster. Ironically, the Bulldogs lost in the first round by a score of 76-56 to Eastern Michigan University.

Four more years would go by before MSU would be invited back to the NCAA playoffs. This time the Bulldogs made it to the third round by defeating Santa Clara, 75-67, and then Utah, 78-64, before losing to UCLA, 86-67. In 1996, the team went all the way to the Final Four before losing. Colvard was rediscovered by CBS Television and interviewed once again about the 1963 miracle team.

By the time the 1963 exploits were revisited twenty years later, Coach McCarthy had died and all the players on that historic team were well into middle age. Leland Mitchell had gone on to play one year of pro ball under McCarthy at New Orleans in the old American Basketball Association, then he had started a real estate business and settled down in Starkville with a wife and children.

Joe Dan Gold had become the head coach at MSU after graduation. He stayed five years before returning to his native Kentucky, where he became the superintendent of Morgan County Schools in West Liberty, Kentucky. Years later Gold would say, "I feel a sense of pride and accomplishment for being a part of that group. We were not a highly recruited group. There were not a lot of blue-chippers, but to be a part of a significant development in the history of a state, I was pleased to be a part of that." After graduating in 1963, Red Stroud played and coached with McCarthy at New Orleans before deciding to be a high school teacher and coach in several locations, finally settling in Morton, Mississippi. Doug Hutton, the 5'-10" sparkplug from Clinton, had ended up as a high school coach in his old hometown. Bobby Shows became a Baptist minister in Little Rock, Arkansas. Stan Brinker chose a career as an Air Force officer. Aubrey Nichols went on to law school at Ole Miss and became a lawyer in Columbus, Mississippi, near his hometown of New Hope.

To a man, the former players had vivid memories of the game against Loyola, but claimed that all they ever wanted to do was play basketball and leave the politics to someone else. "It's everyone's dream to play in the NCAA," Gold recalled in an interview twenty years after the game in Michigan. "We were excited about it. We never understood the significance as far as the university or the state. We were just happy to go play."

As for Colvard, he believed the game was a turning point in the life of Mississippi State and paved the way for the peaceful integration of the university three years later. "I'm so happy to see what has happened in Mississippi," he told the Jackson *Clarion-Ledger* in the story recalling the 1963 incident. "I'm so proud of some of the things that have happened down there. It makes me proud to see them."

The trip to Michigan in 1963 became the subject of a documentary film in 2002 called *A Night in March*. Then *Sports Illustrated* resurrected the incident in a major article on March 11, 2003, with the headline, "Ghosts of Mississippi." The subheading said it all: "Forty years ago a courageous college president defied a court order barring Mississippi State from integrated competition and sent his team to face black players in the NCAA tournament." Author Alexander Wolff gave Colvard full credit for having made the decision to defy Mississippi's unwritten law, saying "the central protagonists in this tale would be Colvard, a political and temperamental moderate from North Carolina, and ordinary white Mississippians. Their feelings sit bare and raw in a corpus of documents: the statements, diaries and memoir of Colvard, who alone made the decision to defy the extreme segregationists."

Probably the most impressive turnaround at MSU did not come on the basketball court, however. It came in the form of money raised by the Mississippi State University Development Foundation. After collecting only $12,542.33 in its first full year of operation, the foundation had blossomed handsomely. In the eighth year, collections passed the $1 million mark for the first time. Even after Colvard left MSU, he was involved in fund-raising for the foundation in Starkville. Before he left he had contacted a 1916 MSU graduate, James N. McArthur, in Florida, and McArthur had insisted that the closure of his $1 million contribution be finalized through Colvard. By the end of the century, the foundation had raised more than $190 million to be used for building and programs over and above the university's state appropriations. In 2000, the foundation board of directors approved a new donor recognition program naming the $1 million–to–$5 million category the Dean W. Colvard Founders. The 2002 report listed thirty-eight gifts in this category and twelve in excess of $5 million.

The new direction that Colvard had given to MSU had certainly borne fruit. "Your heritage continues to blossom here," one of his successors, Dr. Donald W. Zacharias, wrote to him in August 1996. "The people on the campus north of us (Ole Miss) are dying with envy, but they are really not our chief competition anymore. They will always be competitors but our true competition is coming from Georgia Tech, Auburn, Texas A&M, the University of Georgia, and places like that."

At the beginning of the new millenium MSU had been transformed from the place that Colvard had first seen. It was ranked thirteenth in the nation in computing power among U.S. universities, and fifty-seventh in the National Science Foundation listing of top public research universities in the nation. Enrollment had reached more than 16,000, including 2,500 African American students.

UNCC

It is to be one of the most creative campuses of its type in the United States. The Charlotte Institute for Technology Innovation will consist of nearly 1 million square feet of laboratory, classroom, and office space on one hundred acres. It has only one function: provide an incubator to nurture high-technology experimentation and design, not in Silicon Valley, but in the heart of the mid-South. The total price tag should reach more than $100 million dollars. The new institute is only one part of a dream for an urban university that a man from the mountains of North Carolina had many years ago when he took the helm as the first chancellor of the University of North Carolina at Charlotte. More than $268 million worth of construction over the first few years of the twenty-first century will help catapult the still young university into what many say is its truly rightful place in history.

Time has brought town and gown together. When the campus was laid out in the early 1960s nine miles northeast of Charlotte's city limits, critics said it was too far away from the city's central business district. Six hundred acres were set aside for the development of the new university. The location was no accident. Planners believed that a center-city campus would be hemmed in and hampered from further growth by high property values of surrounding real estate. The so-called rural location had other attractive benefits: first, it provided a clean slate for planners to design a truly new university; second, it would help spur development in the area; and third, it would provide a central location for commuting students from areas in several surrounding counties.

Another milestone was reached in August 2000 when the Board of Governors reclassified UNCC as a doctoral/research university under the Carnegie Foundation's new system for classifying colleges and universities. As Chancellor James H. Woodward said, "The designation means that UNCC has earned a place among even more distinguished institutions. It is another step toward our ultimate goal of becoming the research university that this area of the Carolinas so obviously needs. The new classification also means that we will be funded as a doctoral university." Woodward continued, "When UNC Charlotte was established . . . , Bonnie Cone, Dean Colvard and a cadre of leading Charlotteans who were staunch advocates of building a public university in this area of the state fully expected the new institution to become a doctoral/research university. They had no idea it would take thirty-five years."

At UNCC, by 2002 enrollment had grown to 18,000, including 3,100 graduate students, and the university had 65,000 living alumni. Enrollment is projected to increase annually through the year 2010, bringing the university a projected student body of more than 25,000. Students come to UNCC from all one hundred counties in North Carolina, each of the fifty United States, and eighty foreign countries.

A doctoral/research intensive university, UNCC comprises seven colleges: the College of Arts and Sciences and six professional colleges —architecture, business administration, education, engineering, information technology, and nursing and health professions. The university offers eighty programs leading to bachelor's degrees, fifty-one master's degree programs, and nine doctoral programs.

UNCC's faculty includes 680 full-time members, with more than 530 holding doctoral degrees. It serves the community, state, and nation through such agencies as the Urban Institute, the C.C. Cameron Center for Applied Research, the Ben Craig Center (a business incubator), the Center for International Studies, the Office of Continuing Education and Extension, the Center for Applied and Professional Ethics, the Center for Engineering Research and Industrial Development, and the 3,200-acre University Research Park, whose resident companies employ more than 25,000 workers. The university's 1,000-acre campus holds fifty-one buildings, including the J. Murrey Atkins Library, which contains more than 875,000 bound volumes, state-of-the-art computer labs, and various special collections.

While Colvard was proud to have had a role in UNCC's development, he emphasized that most of its progress had occurred since he retired on December 31, 1978. In his installation address on March 3, 1967, he had said, "We at Charlotte do not claim yet to have become a fully developed university. On the other hand, let me now make very clear that we intend to build here, and are daily striving to build here, not only a fully developed university, but as soon as possible a great university; and that in doing this we believe we reflect the spirit of the Latin motto adopted by the people of this state in 1883: *Esse Quam Videri*, To Be Rather Than to Seem."

Dean Colvard's work obviously succeeded. At a May 29, 2002, party in advance of Dean Colvard's eighty-ninth birthday, which fell on July 10, more than 150 people were there to hear Chancellor James Woodward announce that the Colvard Administration Building was being renamed the Dean and Martha Colvard Building. Her portrait was already there beside his.

APPENDIX: CONSULTANTS INVOLVED
IN UNCC PLANNING PROCESS

ACADEMIC PLANNING

Architecture: James E. Ambrose, associate professor of architecture, University of Wisconsin at Milwaukee; Lawrence W. Anderson, dean, School of Architecture, Massachusetts Institute of Technology, Cambridge; Richard D. Berry, associate professor of architecture and associate professor of planning, University of Southern California, Los Angeles; Charles P. Graves, dean, School of Architecture, University of Kentucky, Lexington; H. Samuel Kruse, AIA, partner, Watson, Deutschman and Kruse, Miami; B. N. Lacy, dean, School of Architecture, University of Tennessee, Knoxville.

Creative Arts: Robert W. Corrigan, president, California Institute of the Arts, Burbank; Sidney Simon, professor of art history, University of Minnesota, Minneapolis; Gideon Waldrop, dean, the Julliard School, New York.

Physical Education: William Appenzeller, director of the Department of Recreation and Program Sources, University of Colorado, Boulder; Paul Derr, chairman, Department of Physical Education, North Carolina State University, Raleigh; Betty Flinchum, Department of Physical Education, National Education Association, Washington, D.C.; William T. Haskell, President's Council on Physical Fitness, Washington, D.C.; Gerald S. Kenyon, associate professor of physical education, University of Wisconsin, Madison; Edward Mileff, director of health education, National Education Association, Washington, D.C.; Celeste Ulrich, Department of Physical Education, University of North Carolina, Greensboro.

Engineering: Gordon S. Brown, Donald C. Jackson Professor of Engineering, Massachusetts Institute of Technology, Cambridge; W. L. Everett, dean emeritus, College of Engineering, University of Illinois, Urbana; Newman A. Hall, executive director, National Academy of Engineering, Washington, D.C.; Kenneth G. Picha, dean, School of Engineering, University of Massachusetts, Amherst.

Graduate Degrees in Education: E. J. Cain, dean, College of Education, University of Nevada, Reno; James B. Pearson, professor of history, University of Texas, Austin.

Master of Management: Donald J. Hart, president, St. Andrews Presbyterian College, Laurinburg, N.C.; Luther H. Hodges, Jr., senior vice president and city executive, National Carolina National Bank, Charlotte; James F. Kane, dean, College of Business Administration, University of South Carolina, Columbia; William A. Owens, Jr., director, Psychometric Laboratory, University of Georgia, Athens; J. William Stewart, Jr., resident partner, Haskins and Sells, Charlotte.

Biology: Dale Arvey, chairman, Department of Biology, University of the Pacific, Stockton, Calif.; Robert H. Maier, vice chancellor, University of Wisconsin, Green Bay; Donald C. Scott, chairman, Division of Biological Sciences, University of Georgia, Athens.

Chemistry: Henry Freiser, professor of chemistry, University of Arizona, Tucson; L. B. Rogers, professor of chemistry, Purdue University, Lafayette, Ind.; John H. Wotiz, professor of chemistry, Southern Illinois University, Carbondale.

English: Jacob H. Adler, chairman, Department of English, Purdue University, Lafayette, Ind.; Paul B. Blount, chairman, Department of English, Georgia State University, Atlanta; E. Donald Hirsch, chairman, Department of English, University of Virginia, Charlottesville.

Geography: John Fraser Hart, professor of geography, University of Minnesota, Duluth; Henry Hunker, professor of geography, Ohio State University, Columbus; Howard Roepke, professor of geography, University of Illinois, Urbana.

History: Thomas L. Connelly, associate professor of history, University of South Carolina, Columbia; Richard S. Dunn, professor of history, University of Michigan, Ann Arbor; Gaddis Smith, professor of history, Yale University, New Haven, Conn.

Mathematics: Alexander R. Bednarek, professor of mathematics, University of Florida, Gainesville; Emilie Haynsworth, professor of mathematics, Auburn University, Auburn, Ala.; John W. Neuberger, professor of mathematics, Emory University, Atlanta; George Springer, professor of mathematics, Indiana University, Bloomington.

Black Studies: D. W. Bishop, chairman, history department and Black Studies Committee, Fayetteville State College, Fayetteville, N.C.; James

H. Brewer, professor of history, North Carolina Central University, Durham; Gordon Cleveland, professor of political science and chairman, Black Studies Committee, University of North Carolina, Chapel Hill.

ADMINISTRATIVE PLANNING

University Governance: Otis Singletary, executive vice chancellor, University of Texas System, Austin.

Business Affairs: John S. Allen, president, University of South Florida, Tampa; E. E. Davidson, vice president, Oklahoma State University, Stillwater; John M. Evans, vice president for financial affairs, University of Connecticut, Storrs; Vincent Shea, comptroller, University of Virginia, Charlottesville; Joseph Soshnik, comptroller, University of Nebraska, Lincoln.

Student Affairs—Publications Workshop: Wallace Carroll, editor and publisher, *Winston-Salem Journal and Sentinel*, Winston-Salem, N.C.; Jack Claiborne, city editor, the *Charlotte Observer*, Charlotte; Robert Dunham, editor, *Davidsonian*, Davidson College, Davidson, N.C.; Sam Haywood, principal, Independence High School, Charlotte; Gray Lawrence, editor, *Old Gold and Black*, Wake Forest University, Winston-Salem, N.C.; Rolfe Neill, editor, *Philadelphia Daily News*, Philadelphia; Eugene Payne, editorial cartoonist, the *Charlotte Observer*, Charlotte; Darrell Sifford, managing editor, the *Charlotte News*, Charlotte; Sally Upchurch, editor, *Myerspark*, Myers Park High School, Charlotte.

Administrative Council: John Roosevelt Boettiger, executive assistant to the president, Hampshire College, Amherst, Mass.; J. Martin Klotsche, chancellor, University of Wisconsin, Green Bay; Robert H. Maier, vice chancellor, University of Wisconsin, Green Bay.

COMMUNITY-ORIENTED EFFORTS IN PLANNING

Geography in Urban Education Conference: Edgar Bingham, professor of geography, Emory and Henry College, Emory, Va.; Richard Lonsdale, associate professor of geography, University of North Carolina, Chapel Hill; Tom McCartney, chairman, social science, Gaston College, Dallas, N.C.

INDEX